OPPOSING VIEWPOINTS® SERIES

|||| || ||||||| || ||| |||||||||||||||| ||

W9-BWW-265

Censorship

363.31 Censorsh
Barbour, Scott,
Censorship /2010

PROPERTY OF
HIGH POINT PUBLIC LIBRARY
HIGH POINT, N. C. 27261

$27—

Other Books of Related Interest:

Opposing Viewpoints Series

Civil Liberties

At Issue Series

Is Gun Ownership a Right?

Current Controversies Series

Capitalism

"Congress shall make no law . . . abridging the freedom of speech, or of the press."

First Amendment to the U.S. Constitution

The basic foundation of our democracy is the First Amendment guarantee of freedom of expression. The Opposing Viewpoints Series is dedicated to the concept of this basic freedom and the idea that it is more important to practice it than to enshrine it.

OPPOSING VIEWPOINTS® SERIES

Censorship

Scott Barbour, Book Editor

GREENHAVEN PRESS
A part of Gale, Cengage Learning

PROPERTY OF

GALE
CENGAGE Learning™

Detroit • New York • San Francisco • New Haven, Conn • Waterville, Maine • London

GALE
CENGAGE Learning

Christine Nasso, *Publisher*
Elizabeth Des Chenes, *Managing Editor*

© 2010 Greenhaven Press, a part of Gale, Cengage Learning.

Gale and Greenhaven Press are registered trademarks used herein under license.

For more information, contact:
Greenhaven Press
27500 Drake Rd.
Farmington Hills, MI 48331-3535
Or you can visit our Internet site at gale.cengage.com

ALL RIGHTS RESERVED.
No part of this work covered by the copyright herein may be reproduced, transmitted, stored, or used in any form or by any means graphic, electronic, or mechanical, including but not limited to photocopying, recording, scanning, digitizing, taping, Web distribution, information networks, or information storage and retrieval systems, except as permitted under Section 107 or 108 of the 1976 United States Copyright Act, without the prior written permission of the publisher.

For product information and technology assistance, contact us at

Gale Customer Support, 1-800-877-4253
For permission to use material from this text or product, submit all requests online at
www.cengage.com/permissions

Further permissions questions can be emailed to permissionrequest@cengage.com

Articles in Greenhaven Press anthologies are often edited for length to meet page requirements. In addition, original titles of these works are changed to clearly present the main thesis and to explicitly indicate the author's opinion. Every effort is made to ensure that Greenhaven Press accurately reflects the original intent of the authors. Every effort has been made to trace the owners of copyrighted material.

Cover Image copyright © Maurizio Cigognetti/Photographer's Choice RF/Getty Images

LIBRARY OF CONGRESS CATALOGING-IN-PUBLICATION DATA

Censorship / Scott Barbour, book editor.
    p. cm. -- (Opposing viewpoints)
    Includes bibliographical references and index.
    ISBN 978-0-7377-4761-4 (hardcover) -- ISBN 978-0-7377-4762-1 (pbk.)
    1. Censorship--Juvenile literature. 2. Censorship--United States--Juvenile literature. 3. Freedom of speech--Juvenile literature. 4. Internet--Censorship--Juvenile literature. I. Barbour, Scott, 1963-
    Z657.C393 2010
    363.31--dc22
                                                                        2009040557

323.44

Printed in the United States of America
1 2 3 4 5 6 7 14 13 12 11 10

Contents

Why Consider Opposing Viewpoints?   11

Introduction   14

Chapter 1: Should There Be Limits to Free Speech?

Chapter Preface   19

1. The Press Should Be Censored
   During Wartime   21
   Tony Blankley

2. The Press Should Not Be Censored
   During Wartime   32
   Dean Baquet and Bill Keller

3. The Arts Should Be Censored   39
   Ben Shapiro

4. The Arts Should Not Be Censored   44
   Dominic Cooke

5. The Press Should Self-Censor
   Anti-Islamic Views   49
   Haroon Siddiqui

6. The Press Should Not Self-Censor
   Anti-Islamic Views   54
   Flemming Rose

Periodical Bibliography   60

Chapter 2: Should the Internet Be Censored?

Chapter Preface   62

1. Internet Filters Are Effective   64
   Jacob Sullum

2. Internet Filters Are Ineffective   **68**
Matt Villano

3. Laws to Make the Internet Neutral   **74**
Will Endanger Families
Cesar Conda

4. Laws to Make the Internet Neutral Will   **79**
Prevent Censorship
Damian Kulash

5. Laws to Make the Internet Neutral May   **88**
Cause Censorship
Phil Kerpen

Periodical Bibliography   **93**

Chapter 3: Is Free Speech Censored Worldwide?

Chapter Preface   **95**

1. The Internet Is Censored in   **97**
Repressive Countries
Adam B. Kushner

2. Bloggers Evade Internet Censorship   **106**
in Repressive Countries
Richard Seymour

3. China's Internet Censorship Is Effective   **113**
James Fallows

4. China's Internet Censorship Can   **122**
Be Circumvented
April Gu

5. U.S. Companies Are Abetting Internet   **128**
Censorship in China
Jonathan Mirsky

6. U.S. Companies Are Promoting Internet Freedom in China   133
Clyde Wayne Crews Jr. and Peter Suderman

Periodical Bibliography   137

Chapter 4: Is Freedom in the United States Threatened by Censorship?

Chapter Preface   139

1. Books Are Being Banned in the United States   142
Debra Lau Whelan

2. Book Banning Is Declining in the United States   150
Rob Boston

3. Student Speech Should Not Be Censored   156
Debra J. Saunders

4. Student Speech Should Be Censored   161
Daniel Henninger

5. The Proposed Flag Desecration Amendment Is a Threat to Freedom   167
Nat Hentoff

6. The Proposed Flag Desecration Amendment Is Not a Threat to Freedom   172
Bill Frist

7. Regulation of Talk Radio Will Threaten Free Speech   176
Alan Sears

8. Regulation of Talk Radio Will Protect Free Speech   180
Mark Lloyd

Periodical Bibliography   187
For Further Discussion   188
Organizations to Contact   191
Bibliography of Books   199
Index   203

Why Consider Opposing Viewpoints?

> *"The only way in which a human being can make some approach to knowing the whole of a subject is by hearing what can be said about it by persons of every variety of opinion and studying all modes in which it can be looked at by every character of mind. No wise man ever acquired his wisdom in any mode but this."*
>
> *John Stuart Mill*

In our media-intensive culture it is not difficult to find differing opinions. Thousands of newspapers and magazines and dozens of radio and television talk shows resound with differing points of view. The difficulty lies in deciding which opinion to agree with and which "experts" seem the most credible. The more inundated we become with differing opinions and claims, the more essential it is to hone critical reading and thinking skills to evaluate these ideas. Opposing Viewpoints books address this problem directly by presenting stimulating debates that can be used to enhance and teach these skills. The varied opinions contained in each book examine many different aspects of a single issue. While examining these conveniently edited opposing views, readers can develop critical thinking skills such as the ability to compare and contrast authors' credibility, facts, argumentation styles, use of persuasive techniques, and other stylistic tools. In short, the Opposing Viewpoints Series is an ideal way to attain the higher-level thinking and reading skills so essential in a culture of diverse and contradictory opinions.

In addition to providing a tool for critical thinking, Opposing Viewpoints books challenge readers to question their own strongly held opinions and assumptions. Most people form their opinions on the basis of upbringing, peer pressure, and personal, cultural, or professional bias. By reading carefully balanced opposing views, readers must directly confront new ideas as well as the opinions of those with whom they disagree. This is not to simplistically argue that everyone who reads opposing views will—or should—change his or her opinion. Instead, the series enhances readers' understanding of their own views by encouraging confrontation with opposing ideas. Careful examination of others' views can lead to the readers' understanding of the logical inconsistencies in their own opinions, perspective on why they hold an opinion, and the consideration of the possibility that their opinion requires further evaluation.

Evaluating Other Opinions

To ensure that this type of examination occurs, Opposing Viewpoints books present all types of opinions. Prominent spokespeople on different sides of each issue as well as well-known professionals from many disciplines challenge the reader. An additional goal of the series is to provide a forum for other, less known, or even unpopular viewpoints. The opinion of an ordinary person who has had to make the decision to cut off life support from a terminally ill relative, for example, may be just as valuable and provide just as much insight as a medical ethicist's professional opinion. The editors have two additional purposes in including these less known views. One, the editors encourage readers to respect others' opinions—even when not enhanced by professional credibility. It is only by reading or listening to and objectively evaluating others' ideas that one can determine whether they are worthy of consideration. Two, the inclusion of such viewpoints encourages the important critical thinking skill of objectively evaluating an author's credentials and bias. This evaluation will illuminate an author's reasons for taking a particular stance on an issue and will aid in readers' evaluation of the author's ideas.

It is our hope that these books will give readers a deeper understanding of the issues debated and an appreciation of the complexity of even seemingly simple issues when good and honest people disagree. This awareness is particularly important in a democratic society such as ours in which people enter into public debate to determine the common good. Those with whom one disagrees should not be regarded as enemies but rather as people whose views deserve careful examination and may shed light on one's own.

Thomas Jefferson once said that "difference of opinion leads to inquiry, and inquiry to truth." Jefferson, a broadly educated man, argued that "if a nation expects to be ignorant and free . . . it expects what never was and never will be." As individuals and as a nation, it is imperative that we consider the opinions of others and examine them with skill and discernment. The Opposing Viewpoints Series is intended to help readers achieve this goal.

David L. Bender and Bruno Leone,
Founders

Introduction

"Censorship reflects a society's lack of confidence in itself. It is the landmark of an authoritarian regime."

—Potter Stewart,
U.S. Supreme Court justice

"Judicious government censorship is not the enemy of freedom but its guarantor."

—Roger Kimball,
art critic and social commentator

On May 13, 2009, President Barack Obama announced that he would block the release of photographs showing U.S. soldiers abusing prisoners of war in Iraq and Afghanistan. By making this announcement, he reversed a promise he'd made three weeks before when he'd agreed to release the pictures. The president's reversal brought harsh criticism and loud praise, underscoring the stark differences of opinion that exist on the issue of government censorship.

The Department of Defense had been ordered to release the photos in response to a lawsuit by the American Civil Liberties Union (ACLU), an organization that works to uphold the civil liberties of all Americans. The ACLU had requested that the pictures be made public in a 2003 request under the Freedom of Information Act, a law that governs the disclosure of previously unreleased government documents. Its request was denied, and the ACLU filed a lawsuit, eventually prevailing in the courts. The U.S. Court of Appeals for the Second Circuit ordered that the photos be released on May 28, 2009. Obama originally agreed with the order, but changed his mind after he viewed some of the images and consulted with his generals.

The exact content of the photos in question is not known. It is assumed, however, the pictures are similar to the photos leaked to the press in 2004 depicting prisoner abuse at Abu Ghraib prison in Iraq. These images stoked international outrage with their portrayal of prisoners being stacked in human pyramids, menaced by dogs, tied to leashes, and mistreated and humiliated in other ways—all at the hands of their U.S. captors. The ACLU estimates that there may be as many as 2,000 additional unreleased photos of a similar nature, which were gathered during 200 criminal court cases conducted both before and after the release of the Abu Ghraib pictures in 2004.

The ACLU and other civil liberties groups insist that the release of the photos is essential in order to fully inform the public of the conduct of the government. They contend that Obama's reversal is a violation of the promise he made on his first full day in office as president when he stated, "A democracy requires accountability, and accountability requires transparency." Critics insist that Obama is simply continuing the policies of the George W. Bush administration by covering up the abuses of the past. As stated by Amrit Singh, the ACLU lawyer who was responsible for arguing the case, Obama's administration "has essentially become complicit with the torture that was rampant during the Bush years by being complicit in its cover-up."

President Obama and his defenders insist that releasing the photos would shed no additional light on past misdeeds. More importantly, they contend that making the pictures public would provoke an anti-American backlash that could harm the reputation of the nation and put both citizens and soldiers at risk. As John W. Whitehead, founder and president of the Rutherford Institute, a conservative public policy research organization, argues, "If the photos are as pornographic and offensive as those released in 2004, they could well incite riots in Muslim countries and fuel intense anti-American sentiment. Worst of all, they could place American military forces and civilians in greater jeopardy." As proof, Whitehead points out that in the days after the release of the Abu Ghraib photos in 2004, radical Islamists retaliated by beheading American contractor Nicholas Berg and posting video footage of the execution on the Internet.

Opponents of Obama's decision argue that fear of anti-American sentiment does not justify the squelching of information. In a letter to President Obama, the ACLU, Human Rights Watch, and over twenty-five other civil rights organizations expressed this view: "Suppressing information to prevent public anger is inconsistent with democratic principles. . . . In the end, full disclosure of the crimes committed by our government will make us all safer." Others go further and reject the view that releasing the images will place U.S. soldiers at risk. As stated by Abderrahim Sabir, a spokesman for Human Rights Watch, "U.S. soldiers are at war and they are harmed as a result of war, not the photos." Still others maintain that keeping the photos secret will provoke more bloodshed than releasing them. "Until they're made public, they seem likely only to inflame the imaginations of America's friends and enemies," the *Los Angeles Times* contends. "The worst will be assumed."

The debate over the prisoner abuse photos gets to the heart of the issue of censorship. On one hand, the public has a keen interest in publishing and receiving information about its government and its actions. On the other hand, governments often desire to withhold information to protect its citizens, defend its borders, or in the case of authoritarian regimes, simply to retain power. This tension—between the public's urge for the free exchange of views and the government's need to control information—underlies the viewpoints contained in *Opposing Viewpoints: Censorship*, which contains the following chapters: "Should There Be Limits to Free Speech?" "Should the Internet Be Censored?" "Is

Free Speech Censored Worldwide?" and "Is Freedom in the United States Threatened by Censorship?" Throughout these chapters, authors debate the state of freedom of speech and the use of censorship in the United States and around the world.

OPPOSING
VIEWPOINTS®
SERIES

CHAPTER 1

Should There Be Limits to Free Speech?

Chapter Preface

At the 2002 Billboard Music Awards, broadcast live on Fox, the performer Cher used the f-word while challenging her critics. The following year, at the 2003 Billboard awards, actress Nicole Richie used profanity, including the f-word and s-word, when describing her television show. That same year at the Golden Globe Awards, Bono, the lead singer of the rock band U2, used the f-word while accepting an award. In response to these and other incidents, the Federal Communications Commission (FCC), the government agency responsible for regulating the nation's airwaves, created a rule banning the use of "fleeting expletives"—indecent language aired unintentionally during live broadcasts.

Fox challenged the FCC rule, and on April 28, 2009, the U.S. Supreme Court upheld the ban on fleeting expletives. The Court, however, addressed only the issue of whether the FCC followed correct procedure in making the rule; it did not consider the First Amendment implications of the expletive ban. Therefore, the constitutionality of the ban on fleeting expletives still remains unresolved.

The FCC rule is predicated on the idea that censoring indecent speech is justified on the grounds that it protects children from inappropriate content. Throughout history, the courts have ruled that censoring indecent speech is constitutional. As summed up by *Wall Street Journal* reporters Jess Bravin and Amy Schatz, "Indecent language is defined as involving sexual or excretory functions depicted in a way that is 'patently offensive' to 'contemporary community standards.' Although adults have a constitutional right to indecent materials, courts have upheld government's authority to keep it from children."

Many critics, however, believe the FCC's fleeting expletives rule will eventually be struck down on First Amendment grounds. In a 2007 decision on the same case, the Second Circuit Court of Appeals stated, "We are skeptical that the [FCC] can provide a reasoned explanation for its 'fleeting expletive' regime that would pass constitutional muster." Among other problems, the court found that the FCC's definition of indecency was "undefined, indiscernible, inconsistent, and consequently, unconstitutionally vague."

The debate over fleeting expletives is just one example of conflicting views on what limits should be placed on speech. Other areas of debate include the censorship of sensitive information during wartime, censorship of the arts, and regulations on speech that is deemed offensive to racial, ethnic, or religious minorities. These are among the issues debated in the following chapter.

> *"In order to help prosecute the current war on Islamic fascists, we need some small, reasonable restrictions on the media."*

The Press Should Be Censored During Wartime

Tony Blankley

In the following viewpoint, columnist Tony Blankley argues that the media have been irresponsible in their coverage of the war on terror. For example, he contends that newspapers and broadcast news outlets have exposed secret antiterror operations, thus jeopardizing the government's ability to pursue the nation's enemies. To prevent such misdeeds, Blankley insists the media should be subjected to censorship during wartime, as was done during previous major wars in American history, including the Civil War and both world wars.

As you read, consider the following questions:

1. In what ways were the media censored during World War II, according to the author?

Tony Blankley, *American Grit: What It Will Take to Survive and Win in the 21st Century.* Washington, DC: Regnery, 2009. Copyright © 2009 Tony Blankley. All rights reserved. Reproduced by special permission of Regnery Publishing Inc., Washington DC.

2. As described by Tony Blankley, how did the report from the *New York Times* on the National Security Agency's surveillance operations impede the war on terror?

3. What information did the *Los Angeles Times* reveal in December 2007, as reported by Blankley?

In my previous book, *The West's Last Chance*, I outlined some of the powers assumed by the government under President Roosevelt during World War II. Primary among these powers was the authority FDR [Franklin Delano Roosevelt] gave to FBI director J. Edgar Hoover to censor all news and communications entering or leaving America. A federal Office of Censorship was created to review and if necessary censor any criticism of the morale of U.S. forces, or any communication that might bring aid or comfort to the enemy. Censorship applied not only to news and commentary, but also popular entertainment. Antiwar films were all but unheard of, since the government simply would not allow them.

There is a marked contrast between that situation and what we see today, when the American public has been treated to a parade of Hollywood antiwar films, including *Rendition*, *Lions for Lambs*, *Stop-Loss*, and *Redacted*, to name a few. Notwithstanding liberal hyperventilating over the supposed infringements on their right to "dissent," Americans remain free to denounce the government, the war effort, and the U.S. military in the most disparaging terms, which is typically what one sees in the antiwar rallies that occur every few months on the Washington Mall, with the full permission of the authorities.

Notwithstanding his current status as a liberal icon, President Roosevelt was not particularly liberal about tolerating dissent during wartime, repeatedly asking his Attorney General, Francis Biddle, "When are you going to indict the seditionists?" Fascists, Communists, and isolationists were prosecuted or denaturalized for speaking out against the war effort.

Most notable among these repressions was the case against William Dudley Pelley, an isolationist and Nazi sympathizer who spent ten years in jail after being convicted of seditious libel for his denunciations of the war and of Roosevelt personally.

At the beginning of World War II, around twenty-six news stories were censored in the American press every day; by the end of 1942, the post office had completely outlawed seventy newspapers. Compare that restrictive environment to the laxity that prevails today, when the *Washington Post*, absolutely unhindered by the government, prints op-ed submissions by the likes of Mahmoud al-Zahar, a founder and top official of Hamas, which is a U.S.-designated terrorist organization, and Mousa Abu Marzook, a Hamas terrorist who is listed as a specially designated terrorist by the U.S. Treasury Department. Similarly, a Web site run by the *Washington Post* and *Newsweek* saw fit to run a piece on the meaning of jihad written by Muhammad Hussein Fadlallah, a spiritual leader of Hezbollah, another U.S.-designated terrorist organization. U.S. intelligence agents have suspected Fadlallah of helping to organize Hezbollah's 1983 suicide bombing attack on the Marine barracks in Beirut that killed 241 U.S. servicemen.

It is hard to imagine the population on the home front during World War II waking up one morning, opening the paper, and finding a direct appeal to the American people from a top official from Nazi Germany's Propaganda Ministry, or an entreaty from an Imperial Japanese pilot suspected of participating in the attack on Pearl Harbor. And yet, ignoring the unarguable success of censorship policies in maintaining morale and protecting state secrets throughout the long days of World War II, liberals and libertarians incessantly bemoan the few, commonsense restrictions on civil liberties that the government has taken since September 11, denouncing them as abhorrent measures ushering in a totalitarian state.

The *New York Times*, naturally, led the charge, deploring parts of the Patriot Act for providing "license for federal agents to spy on innocent people and suppress dissent." Tellingly, the paper declined to specify exactly whose right to dissent is being squelched. Joe Conason added this dire warning: "In America, where traditions of free expression and government accountability remain strong, such centralized power over the means of expression cannot easily be achieved—not even in wartime. Yet that difficulty hasn't discouraged the Republican regime from seeking *unprecedented* power over what we can see, hear, and read about our rulers and their policies."

To the contrary, the "Republican regime" did not seek out anything even remotely approaching the kind of censorship power that Roosevelt exerted during World War II. What's more, Roosevelt's policies themselves were hardly unprecedented. Those *New York Times* editors who see the Patriot Act as a powerful weapon against dissent should compare the act's actual stipulations to the kind of restrictions that President Wilson enacted during World War I. The section of the Patriot Act that the *Times* most vociferously attacked was the now-revoked stipulation permitting the government to access the library records of terrorism suspects. And indeed, allowing FBI agents to ascertain which books a terrorism suspect checked out did represent a new wartime restriction on civil liberties. But let's compare this authority to the kinds of powers claimed by the government during World War I. As Jonah Goldberg relates,

> Even as the government was churning out propaganda, it was silencing dissent. Wilson's Sedition Act banned "uttering, printing, writing, or publishing any disloyal, profane, scurrilous, or abusive language about the United States government or the military." The postmaster general was given the authority to deny mailing privileges to any publication he saw fit—effectively shutting it down. At least seventy-five periodicals were banned. Foreign publications were not al-

lowed unless their content was first translated and approved by censors. Journalists also faced the very real threat of being jailed or having their supply of newsprint terminated by the War Industries Board.

These policies were not dissimilar from those that had been adopted by President Lincoln. During the Civil War, not only were all telegraph messages subject to censorship, but the government also shut down dozens of newspapers and imprisoned their editors. Thousands of people were arrested for "disloyalty." Most famously, Lincoln suspended habeas corpus, allowing for the temporary abolition of normal legal procedures for suspected criminals.

This is not to defend every wartime restriction approved by American presidents, or to imply that all these policies are needed today. I relate this history to make the point that in America's past, it was well understood by people of all political persuasions that in periods of wartime, when the nation faces a heightened national security threat, the government can and should exert certain powers that are not exercised during peacetime. As a trio of liberal advisors opined to the Roosevelt administration in a communication justifying the evacuation of ethnic Japanese from the West Coast, "In time of national peril any reasonable doubt must be resolved in favor of action to preserve the national safety, not for the purpose of punishing those whose liberty may be temporarily affected by such action, but for the purpose of protecting the freedom of the nation which may be long impaired, if not permanently lost, by non-action."

The Media's Endangerment of America

In order to help prosecute the current war on Islamic fascists, we need some small, reasonable restrictions on the media. This should not, by any means, impinge on any media outlet's ability to editorialize for or against the war; most of the mainstream media have lined up against the war in Iraq, and op-

Change First Amendment Protections

We need an expeditious review of current domestic law to see what changes can be made within the protections of the First Amendment to ensure that free speech protection claims are not used to protect the advocacy of terrorism, violent conduct or the killing of innocents.

Newt Gingrich,
"The First Amendment Is Not a Suicide Pact,"
American Enterprise Institute,
December 8, 2006. www.aei.org.

posed nearly all of President Bush's national security policies. That is their right. But there is no reason why newspapers should remain free to publish direct appeals to the American public from members of designated terrorist organizations. Likewise, misguided activists like former president Jimmy Carter, who ignored warnings from the State Department and met with the Hamas leadership in Syria in an attempt to supplant the government's diplomatic program with his own, should be held to account by having his passport revoked—at a minimum.

Most important, the media should not enjoy the unfettered right to publish national security, intelligence, and military secrets. These revelations can be so damaging to national security that sanctions should be enforced not just against government officials who leak secrets, but also against the journalists and media outlets that disclose them. Currently, this remains a gray area in the law, with various court precedents protecting the media's right to publish secrets, while others have affirmed the government's right to forbid the publication of classified information if it would cause "grave and irreparable" danger.

This kind of danger was certainly caused by the *New York Times*'s 2005 revelation of the National Security Agency's terrorist surveillance program. This secret program, a key tool in the war against Islamic terrorism, monitored communications between U.S.-based terrorism suspects and their foreign contacts. Although a judge later ruled the program illegal because the government did not seek warrants from the Foreign Intelligence Surveillance Act (FISA) courts for its wiretaps, that decision was later overturned. Nevertheless, in the meantime the government began petitioning for warrants to the FISA court, which proceeded to proclaim jurisdiction over the surveillance of foreign-based terrorism suspects merely if they used American communications networks.

Congress countered the FISA court's power grab by approving most elements of the original terrorist surveillance program. But this provided little solace to National Security Agency agents, whose surveillance efforts had been compromised by the leak to the *New York Times*. Once terrorists know they're being monitored—and even *how* they're being monitored—the effectiveness of the surveillance is severely degraded.

Critics falsely claimed that the terrorist surveillance program was illegal. As lawyer David Rivkin notes, the president is vested with the constitutional authority to order electronic surveillance of both domestic- and foreign-based enemies during wartime. But even if the program had been illegal, this would still not justify the revelation of its existence in the press. The United States already has firm procedures—codified in the Intelligence Community Whistleblower Protection Act of 1998—for whistleblowers to bring acts of malfeasance involving intelligence matters to Congress's attention. It is illegal for intelligence agents to leak this information to the press, and it should be illegal for the press to reveal it to the public.

Barack Obama surprised and disappointed a lot of his supporters in 2008 when he voted in favor of a FISA reform bill that provided retroactive immunity to telecom companies that were sued for cooperating with the terrorist surveillance program. While he deserves credit for voting to quash these politically motivated lawsuits, the depth of Obama's conviction is questionable, to say the least. His vote came shortly after he became the presumptive Democratic nominee in the presidential election, at a time when he was moving to the center on many issues. Until just weeks before his FISA vote, Obama had proudly worked with other Democrats to block immunity for telecom companies, threatening to filibuster any bill that included the measure. He declared, "I am proud to stand with Senator [Christopher] Dodd, Senator [Russ] Feingold and a grassroots movement of Americans who are refusing to let President Bush put protections for special interests ahead of our security and our liberty. There is no reason why telephone companies should be given blanket immunity to cover violations of the rights of the American people." And soon after, Obama voted to do precisely that.

The fecklessness of politicians on this issue, and their focus on imaginary violations of civil liberties instead of the real scandal of media complicity in disclosing national secrets, has allowed this unacceptable situation to continue. Having faced no legal consequences for revealing the terrorist surveillance program, the *New York Times* was emboldened to repeat its shameful performance. In 2006, the *Times* and other newspapers published details of another secret antiterrorism surveillance program, this one aimed at monitoring terrorism suspects' international banking transactions. President Bush denounced the program's disclosure as "disgraceful," declaring, "We're at war with a bunch of people who want to hurt the United States of America, and for people to leak that program, and for a newspaper to publish it, does great harm to the United States of America."

Republican Congressman Peter T. King of New York called for the prosecution of the *Times* for treason, but the Justice

Department declined to press charges. Thus, the president was left impotent as the media undermined another key tool for fighting terrorists.

It's clear that appeals to the media's sense of patriotism will fall on deaf ears. During the Bush years, the media blissfully endangered America's safety for the pleasure of striking a blow at a president they despised. The administration had asked the *Times* not to disclose the banking surveillance program, explaining how its revelation would damage national security. But the *Times* editors imperiously dismissed the administration's concerns, arguing without any factual basis that terrorist financiers already knew their transactions were being monitored. In defending the paper's actions, the *Times* executive editor Bill Keller did not make any specific allegations of illegality or impropriety against the program, instead citing the "discomfort" over its legality and oversight allegedly felt by "some" anonymous "officials." Keller also trumpeted the *Times*'s role as a government watchdog, proclaiming that "the people who invented this country saw an aggressive, independent press as a protective measure against the abuse of power in a democracy, and an essential ingredient for self-government."

As a matter of general principle, that is true enough. But I have yet to find a statement from any of the Founding Fathers defending the press's right to publish state secrets during wartime. It was only because the Bush administration was so much less authoritarian than the administration of Abraham Lincoln or Woodrow Wilson or Franklin Delano Roosevelt that the *Times*'s right to publish was permitted to trump national security concerns. The Bush administration should have responded to the *New York Times*'s gross irresponsibility by prosecuting journalists, editors, and publishers who endanger the public by revealing secret antiterrorism programs. As then White House press secretary Tony Snow remarked at the time, "the *New York Times* and other news organizations ought to think long and hard about whether a public's right to know, in some cases, might overwrite somebody's right to live."

Even when there's absolutely no allegation of wrongdoing, it seems that many newspapers today take a perverse pride in revealing U.S. intelligence secrets. In December 2007, the *L.A. Times* revealed the existence of a secret CIA program to entice officials working on Iran's nuclear program to defect. The paper, citing anonymous current and former U.S. intelligence officials, described the effort as "part of a major intelligence push against Iran" designed to gain a more accurate understanding of Iran's nuclear activities and to hinder Iranian efforts to develop a nuclear weapon.

What possible justification exists for allowing the *L.A. Times* to sabotage a vital intelligence program against one of the world's top sponsors of international terrorism? Iran's nuclear development program is one of the most dangerous foreign policy challenges that we face today. Secret operations to subvert or impede Iran's development of nuclear weapons make the world a safer place and lessen the chances of war and nuclear terrorism. Yet, for the *L.A. Times*, considerations of national security take a back seat to the glory gained from publishing a big scoop.

This problem is not confined to newspapers. Yet another damaging leak occurred in October 2007, when the ABC News Web site posted clips from a new al Qaeda video featuring Osama bin Laden. It turns out that the U.S. government had penetrated the al Qaeda Internet communications system, known as Obelisk, and gotten hold of the video before al Qaeda had released it to the public. However, someone leaked the video to ABC News, whose Internet broadcast of the video tipped off al Qaeda that its communications system had been compromised. Unsurprisingly, al Qaeda then shut down the entire network. Rita Katz, the head of an intelligence group that helps the government monitor terrorist communications on the Internet, explained the consequences: "The government leak damaged our investigation into al Qaeda's network. Techniques and sources that took years to develop became ineffective. As a result of the leak al Qaeda changed their methods." A U.S. intelligence official added, "We saw the whole thing [Obelisk] shut down because of this leak. . . . We lost an important keyhole into the enemy."

Nearly all mainstream newspapers have been scathing toward the Bush administration for the intelligence failures surrounding Iraq's weapons of mass destruction program. But how can they demand that the U.S. improve its intelligence capabilities when the papers themselves actively undermine them? Tipping off international terrorists that their communications are being monitored, and informing hostile regimes that their officials are targeted as potential defectors, undermines national security while serving no public purpose whatsoever.

> "To publish or not to publish.... Making those decisions is the responsibility that falls to editors.... It is not one we can surrender to the government."

The Press Should Not Be Censored During Wartime

Dean Baquet and Bill Keller

The following viewpoint is written by Dean Baquet, former editor of the Los Angeles Times *and current Washington bureau chief and assistant managing editor of the* New York Times, *and Bill Keller, executive editor of the* New York Times. *Baquet and Keller reject the idea that the government should control news reporting about the war on terror. They concede that news reporters have a responsibility to balance the public's right to information against the government's need for secrecy. They insist, however, the ultimate decision about what to publish must be left to editors, not the government.*

As you read, consider the following questions:

1. According to Hugo Black, as quoted by the authors, why was the government's power to censor abolished?

Dean Baquet and Ben Keller, "When Do We Publish a Secret?" *New York Times*, July 1, 2006, p. A15. Copyright © 2006 by The New York Times Company. Reprinted with permission.

2. In what situations is it easy to decide to withhold information, according to Dean Baquet and Bill Keller?

3. What stories did the *New York Times* hold at the request of government officials, as reported by the authors?

Since Sept. 11, 2001, newspaper editors have faced excruciating choices in covering the government's efforts to protect the country from terrorist agents. Each of us has, on a number of occasions, withheld information because we were convinced that publishing it could put lives at risk. On other occasions, each of us has decided to publish classified information over strong objections from our government.

Last week [June 2006] our newspapers disclosed a secret Bush administration program to monitor international banking transactions. We did so after appeals from senior administration officials to hold the story. Our reports—like earlier press disclosures of secret measures to combat terrorism—revived an emotional national debate, featuring angry calls of "treason" and proposals that journalists be jailed along with much genuine concern and confusion about the role of the press in times like these.

We are rivals. Our newspapers compete on a hundred fronts every day. We apply the principles of journalism individually as editors of independent newspapers. We agree, however, on some basics about the immense responsibility the press has been given by the inventors of the country.

The Job of Journalists

Make no mistake, journalists have a large and personal stake in the country's security. We live and work in cities that have been tragically marked as terrorist targets. Reporters and photographers from both our papers braved the collapsing towers to convey the horror to the world.

We have correspondents today alongside troops on the front lines in Iraq and Afghanistan. Others risk their lives in a quest to understand the terrorist threat; Daniel Pearl of the *Wall Street Journal* was murdered on such a mission. We, and the people who work for us, are not neutral in the struggle against terrorism.

But the virulent hatred espoused by terrorists, judging by their literature, is directed not just against our people and our buildings. It is also aimed at our values, at our freedoms and at our faith in the self-government of an informed electorate. If the freedom of the press makes some Americans uneasy, it is anathema [a thing detested] to the ideologists of terror.

Thirty-five years ago yesterday, in the Supreme Court ruling that stopped the government from suppressing the secret Vietnam War history called the Pentagon Papers, Justice Hugo Black wrote: "The government's power to censor the press was abolished so that the press would remain forever free to censure the government. The press was protected so that it could bare the secrets of the government and inform the people."

As that sliver of judicial history reminds us, the conflict between the government's passion for secrecy and the press's drive to reveal is not of recent origin. This did not begin with the Bush administration, although the polarization of the electorate and the daunting challenge of terrorism have made the tension between press and government as clamorous as at any time since Justice Black wrote.

Our job, especially in times like these, is to bring our readers information that will enable them to judge how well their elected leaders are fighting on their behalf, and at what price.

Government Wants It Both Ways

In recent years our papers have brought you a great deal of information the White House never intended for you to know—classified secrets about the questionable intelligence that led the country to war in Iraq, about the abuse of prisoners in Iraq and Afghanistan, about the transfer of suspects to countries that are not squeamish about using torture, about eavesdropping without warrants.

As Robert G. Kaiser, associate editor of the *Washington Post*, asked recently in the pages of that newspaper: "You may have been shocked by these revelations, or not at all disturbed by them, but would you have preferred not to know them at all? If a war is being waged in America's name, shouldn't Americans understand how it is being waged?"

Government officials, understandably, want it both ways. They want us to protect their secrets, and they want us to trumpet their successes. A few days ago, Treasury Secretary John Snow said he was scandalized by our decision to report on the bank-monitoring program. But in September 2003 the same Secretary Snow invited a group of reporters from our papers, the *Wall Street Journal* and others to travel with him and his aides on a military aircraft for a six-day tour to show off the department's efforts to track terrorist financing. The secretary's team discussed many sensitive details of their monitoring efforts, hoping they would appear in print and demonstrate the administration's relentlessness against the terrorist threat.

Deciding When to Inform

How do we, as editors, reconcile the obligation to inform with the instinct to protect?

Sometimes the judgments are easy. Our reporters in Iraq and Afghanistan, for example, take great care not to divulge operational intelligence in their news reports, knowing that in this wired age it could be seen and used by insurgents.

Often the judgments are painfully hard. In those cases, we cool our competitive jets and begin an intensive deliberative process.

The process begins with reporting. Sensitive stories do not fall into our hands. They may begin with a tip from a source who has a grievance or a guilty conscience, but those tips are just the beginning of long, painstaking work. Reporters operate without security clearances, without subpoena powers,

Printing Truth for the People

It is not for the press but for the people that we fight for access to the corridors of power, as the people's surrogates. It is not for the press but for the people that we pressure our elected representatives and our candidates for office to answer the questions that the people might ask, if they had the opportunity. And it is not for the press but for the people that we defend (and call for our publishers and news owners to defend) our right to print and broadcast the truth.

Dan Rather,
Remarks at the National Coalition Against Censorship's
Annual Celebration of Free Speech and Its Defendants,
October 21, 2008. www.ncac.org.

without spy technology. They work, rather, with sources who may be scared, who may know only part of the story, who may have their own agendas that need to be discovered and taken into account. We double-check and triple-check. We seek out sources with different points of view. We challenge our sources when contradictory information emerges.

Then we listen. No article on a classified program gets published until the responsible officials have been given a fair opportunity to comment. And if they want to argue that publication represents a danger to national security, we put things on hold and give them a respectful hearing. Often, we agree to participate in off-the-record conversations with officials, so they can make their case without fear of spilling more secrets onto our front pages.

Finally, we weigh the merits of publishing against the risks of publishing. There is no magic formula, no neat metric for either the public's interest or the dangers of publishing sensitive information. We make our best judgment.

Examples of Holding Articles

When we come down in favor of publishing, of course, everyone hears about it. Few people are aware when we decide to hold an article. But each of us, in the past few years, has had the experience of withholding or delaying articles when the administration convinced us that the risk of publication outweighed the benefits. Probably the most discussed instance was the *New York Times*'s decision to hold its article on telephone eavesdropping for more than a year, until editors felt that further reporting had whittled away the administration's case for secrecy.

But there are other examples. The *New York Times* has held articles that, if published, might have jeopardized efforts to protect vulnerable stockpiles of nuclear material, and articles about highly sensitive counterterrorism initiatives that are still in operation. In April [2006], the *Los Angeles Times* withheld information about American espionage and surveillance activities in Afghanistan discovered on computer drives purchased by reporters in an Afghan bazaar.

It is not always a matter of publishing an article or killing it. Sometimes we deal with the security concerns by editing out gratuitous detail that lends little to public understanding but might be useful to the targets of surveillance. The *Washington Post*, at the administration's request, agreed not to name the specific countries that had secret Central Intelligence Agency prisons, deeming that information not essential for American readers. The *New York Times*, in its article on National Security Agency eavesdropping, left out some technical details.

Even the banking articles, which the president and vice president have condemned, did not dwell on the operational or technical aspects of the program, but on its sweep, the questions about its legal basis and the issues of oversight.

We understand that honorable people may disagree with any of these choices—to publish or not to publish. But making those decisions is the responsibility that falls to editors, a corollary to the great gift of our independence. It is not a responsibility we take lightly. And it is not one we can surrender to the government.

> "The public has an interest in preventing the pollution of its artistic culture—and the law should reflect that interest."

The Arts Should Be Censored

Ben Shapiro

In the following viewpoint, columnist Ben Shapiro argues that laws must be enacted to set limits on free artistic expression. He cites several examples of artists whose unbound "free expression" has crossed the boundaries of acceptable public expression. Unless regulations are enacted, he insists, artists will continue to create art that is obscene, vulgar, and demeaning to human beings. Moreover, he fears that this "art" will become the norm, to the detriment of the culture at large.

As you read, consider the following questions:

1. How does Ben Shapiro describe Aliza Shvarts's so-called art project?

2. What rights besides artistic freedom have limits, according to Shapiro?

Ben Shapiro, "No Bodily Fluids in the Public Square," Human Events.com, April 24, 2008. Copyright © 2008 Human Events Inc. Reproduced by permission.

3. Who were some of the past artists that flourished despite the imposition of restrictions on free expression, as noted by the author?

Art, they say, is in the eye of the beholder. No one has come up with a workable definition of art that can universally separate garbage like Karen Finley's body goo[1] from Michelangelo's *David*. And because art is so difficult, so amorphous and difficult to define, civilized people have shied away from attempting to place limits on it. The best policy, we have decided, is to allow everything into the artistic marketplace, and let history and time sort it all out.

There's only one problem with this strategy: If you pollute the artistic marketplace with unmitigated crap, no one will want to visit the marketplace. Art itself will die, or at least be relegated to the few, proud elitists who busily wade through mountains of manure, proclaiming it intellectual gold.

The Need for Limits

Art thrives most when it has reasonable limits. When there are no hard limits, artists who push the envelope are given the most attention. Those "artists" attract the most imitators. And so the "artist" who drops a crucifix in a jar of urine [a reference to a work by photographer Andres Serrano] breeds the "artist" who douses herself in chocolate syrup [Finley]. The "artist" who douses herself in chocolate syrup breeds the "artist" who engages in acts of sodomy before a live audience [a reference to the play *The Romans in Britain*, which contains a scene in which a man rapes another man].

And all of these artists breed the "artist" who supposedly artificially inseminates herself, induces her own miscarriages, films those miscarriages, saves the blood, mixes it with Vaseline, spreads the mixture on saran wrap and then projects the video of her miscarriages onto the saran wrap screen.

1. Karen Finley is a controversial performance artist whose shows have included smearing her body with chocolate and other substances.

Jesse Helms Versus the National Endowment for the Arts

When the National Endowment for the Arts (NEA) came up for a five-year budget review in 1989, it came under fire from Sen. Jesse Helms, a conservative Republican from North Carolina. Helms was outraged that taxpayers were (indirectly) helping to fund art that he and many other religious conservatives considered indecent. One example he cited was an exhibit of photographs by Robert Mapplethorpe (who had recently [March 9, 1989] died of an AIDS-related illness) that featured homoerotic and sadomasochistic imagery. The second, a traveling show organized by the Southeastern Center for Contemporary Art, featured *Piss Christ*, a photograph by Andres Serrano that showed a crucifix submerged in a glass of the artist's urine. Helms introduced an appropriation bill that would ban the NEA or any other federal agency from funding "obscene" art. . . .

The Senate found Helms's definition of indecency too vague and too broad to implement and voted down his bill 62-35. In its place they suggested a compromise: the NEA would adopt the obscenity guidelines set by the Supreme Court in 1973, when it ruled that individual communities should set standards by which to judge the artistic merit of a work. This way certain obscene art could be denied funding, but at the discretion of the NEA, not Congress. Helms did not lose his battle altogether, however. Congress cut NEA funding by $45,000, the exact amount of the original grants for the Mapplethorpe exhibit and the Serrano show.

Gale Research, "Culture Wars in the 1980s,"
Discovering U.S. History. *Farmington Hills, MI: Gale, 1997.*

Last week [April 2008], a national furor arose over Yale student Aliza Shvarts's "art" project, which contemplated doing just that: projecting abortion videos onto abortion leftovers. The political right was understandably outraged—the immorality of the abortions is sick-making on its own. The political left was, somewhat puzzlingly, also perturbed—they condemned Shvarts's "approach and presentation," though one struggles to see their problem, considering Shvarts's repeated abortions are legal only due to their adamant support for abortion-on-demand.

The Art World's Response

The art world was largely silent on Shvarts's project. They were not silent, however, on the prospect of censorship. "Public media has been practicing vigilant self-censorship ever since (Sept. 11, 2001)—in my opinion, a very irresponsible choice," said performance artist, Yale lecturer and probable Shvarts-advisor Pia Lindman. "I am still waiting for this self-aggrandizing mass psychosis; the uncritical belief in the omnipotence and goodness of the American people, troops and government, to dissolve and have it replaced with sober self-reflection."

Cary Nelson of the American Association of University Professors was more circumspect: "Academic freedom for faculty and intellectual freedom for students give them the right to speech that shocks and challenges." Helaine S. Klasky, spokeswoman for Yale, stated, "The entire project is an art piece, a creative fiction designed to draw attention to the ambiguity surrounding form and function of a woman's body. (Shvarts) is an artist and has the right to express herself through performance art."

All rights have reasonable limits. The right to bear arms does not include a right to own a nuclear weapon. The right to free exercise of religion does not include a right to ritualistic child sacrifice. The right to free expression in art should not include a right to film yourself having an abortion; neither should it include a right to use feces, urine or any other bodily fluid in public, nor should it include a right to engage in sex acts before live audiences.

The public has an interest in preventing the pollution of its artistic culture—and the law should reflect that interest. As for the "boundary-pushing" performance "artists," those "artists" who cannot work within the bounds of common decency should find another line of work. [William] Shakespeare somehow worked within the strict guidelines of his time; so did da Vinci, and so did Beethoven, Brahms, Bach and Mozart. If Aliza Shvarts, Robert Mapplethorpe [a controversial photographer whose work is sometimes sexually explicit], Andres Serrano and other "artists" cannot do the same, they ought to consider going into the demolition business. After all, they're so good at destroying worthwhile ideas and limits already.

> *"Artists have a right—and sometimes a duty—to offend their audiences."*

The Arts Should Not Be Censored

Dominic Cooke

Dominic Cooke is an English theatre director, playwright, and the artistic director of the Royal Court Theatre in London. In the following viewpoint, he argues that while official censorship of the arts has decreased, a dangerous self-censorship has taken its place. He notes several attempts by fundamentalist religious groups to censor art they consider offensive. These efforts, he believes, have led artists to stifle their own views out of fear of offending overly sensitive religious groups, thus diminishing the power of their art to provoke thought and dialogue on important issues.

As you read, consider the following questions:

1. How did William Gaskill evade the censors, according to the author?

2. Why is Terence Koh's exhibition controversial, as reported by Dominic Cooke?

Dominic Cooke, "An Insidious Form of Censorship," *Spectator*, October 11, 2008, p. 49. Copyright © 2008 by The Spectator. Reproduced by permission of The *Spectator*.

3. How do liberals complicate the issue of self-censorship of the arts, as explained by the author?

Forty years ago, the Theatres Bill removed from the Lord Chamberlain [the senior officer of the Royal Household] his centuries-old power to censor the British stage. Under a law unchanged since 1843, every work intended for production in British theatres had first to be submitted to, and approved by, his office. Each work came back with a report from one of the censors, who became renowned for their hypersensitive ability to read sex and subversion into the most innocent of dialogue. Kenneth Tynan quotes some choice reports in his famous 1965 polemic *The Royal Smut-Hound*: the phrase 'balls of the Medici' is banned, for example (although the report does give the helpful suggestion that 'testicles of the Medici' would be acceptable). Another personal favourite, also quoted by Tynan, is the following masterpiece of straight-faced absurdity: 'Page 14: Omit "the perversions of rubber". Substitute "the kreurpels and blinges of the rubber". Omit the chamber pot under the bed.'

As well as Tynan, the Royal Court Theatre, under its artistic director William Gaskill, fought bitterly against the Lord Chamberlain's office, even, on occasion, openly flouting the censor's demands. At performances of Edward Bond's *Early Morning*, Royal Court patrons were charged a 'membership fee' on the door, rather than being sold a ticket, thereby exploiting a loophole which exempted private theatre clubs from censorship.

Aside from the more comical aberrations of the censor's pencil, there is, of course, a sinister side to the limiting of freedom of speech by a government-appointed official. Peter Hall has written wisely about the function of censorship as 'a means of exerting power, preventing debate and discouraging challenge'. It is a despicable form of bullying, made all the more hurtful and infuriating when legitimised by the state, or other institutions.

Used with permission of Ann Telnaes and the Cartoonist Group. All rights reserved.

At last, in September 1968, common sense prevailed and the law was changed. The single biggest limit on the freedom of expression in British theatre was abolished, and new worlds of possibilities opened up to writers and directors.

The Danger of Self-Censorship

But censorship remains. A whole generation of playwrights has grown old without the amendments of the blue pencil, but the limits placed on our speech now come not from the government, but from our own fear of repercussion in the face of religious extremism. Artists have a right—and sometimes a duty—to offend their audiences. And audiences have a right—and sometimes a duty—to be offended by what they see or hear. But when it is generally assumed that an audience has a right not to be offended, then the restrictions imposed upon an artist are just as stifling as the Lord Chamberlain's.

I say this because Terence Koh's recent exhibition, which includes a statue of Christ with an erection, has re-inflamed the debate about the rights and wrongs of art which offends. I have not seen the exhibition, but I support the Baltic Centre in presenting it. The ongoing battle against the suppression of free expression will not be won by fearing to cause offence. Nevertheless, it is true that sometimes the reaction to a piece will deny it the chance of a fair appraisal, necessitating a painful act of self-censorship on the part of arts programmers.

One does not need an encyclopaedic knowledge of British culture to be able to name an example of modern attempts at censorship. The fatwa against Salman Rushdie, the pickets outside *Jerry Springer—The Opera*, the violent protests against *Behzti* at the Birmingham Repertory Theatre.[1] In all these cases, religious fundamentalists have attempted and, in the example of Birmingham, won their attempt to deny freedom of expression to artists, and to audiences the opportunity to make up their own minds.

Of course, the claims are specious. To fear that a centuries-old faith might be endangered by one play, or that a person's strongly held beliefs may be devalued by somebody else disagreeing, or even satirising them, reveals a hatred of plurality that is common to all fascist ideologies. However, it is made more complex by the fact that many liberals, out of a fear of appearing racist, and with shared sympathy for many of the political causes that also motivate those with a fundamentalist agenda turn a blind eye to such intolerance.

Examples such as the ones above are rare. And the groups that cause them are small, and led by literalists rather than the majority of religious believers. Nevertheless, such actions, especially when successful, foster fear in artistic organisations of the possible ramifications of producing work that criticises re-

1. In 1989, the Ayatollah Khomeini, the leader of Iran, issued a fatwa, or religious decree, calling for the death of author Salman Rushdie for his book *The Satanic Verses*, which he deemed blasphemous toward Islam. In 2005, *Jerry Springer—The Opera*, a musical comedy based on the *Jerry Springer* TV show, was deemed blasphemous by Christian groups. In 2004, riots broke out on opening night of *Behzti*, a play that was viewed as offensive to Sikhs, leading to cancellation of the play.

ligion. This is a profoundly insidious form of censorship, unspoken and therefore hard to criticise.

A Self-Perpetuating Climate of Fear

Sometimes this is a result of a genuine safety threat posed to arts organisations. The management of Birmingham Rep, faced with credible threats of violence against their staff, and without adequate protection from the police, had no choice but to pull *Behzti*. I do not blame them for that. But I believe we are in danger of reaching a situation where a fear of offending has become so internalised and automatic that it isn't even noticed. It may appear well intentioned, but it is no less harmful to free speech than the Lord Chamberlain. The only way we can establish our boundaries is by testing them, and the overly sensitive suppression of anything that even brushes against those boundaries creates a self-perpetuating climate of fear and timidity.

For once arts organisations cease to present work that might offend, artists will cease to create it. Then the small-minded, the bigoted, and the self-righteous can celebrate their victory, and the arts world can only count its losses.

But every morning when I arrive at work, I long to find in that day's post good plays that are not hampered by fear of what they can and can't say, or by fear of causing offence. Plays like Christopher Shinn's *Now or Later*, which is accurate in its analysis of the complex question of the limits of pluralism and its conflict with fundamentalism. The theatre I run exists to produce exactly those plays. They're out there. They've probably already been written, and I am convinced that there are hundreds of people who could yet write them, even if they have never considered doing so. I want that play, and I want the Royal Court to produce it. And when we do, we may fear the consequences, but if we feel the play can bear it, that certainly wouldn't stop us.

> *"Invoking freedom of speech or the need to puncture political correctness are no more than smokescreens to hide [a] larger, and uglier, truth."*

The Press Should Self-Censor Anti-Islamic Views

Haroon Siddiqui

In September 2005, the Danish daily newspaper Jyllands-Posten *published twelve cartoons depicting the Islamic prophet Muhammad. Muslims strongly opposed the publication of the cartoons, while the newspaper's editors defended their decision on the basis of freedom of speech. In the following viewpoint, Haroon Siddiqui, editor emeritus of the* Toronto Star, *a daily newspaper in Toronto, Canada, condemns the publication of the cartoons as a deliberate attempt to provoke Muslims. He concludes that despite the right to free speech, journalists have a responsibility to refrain from publishing material that will incite social conflict.*

As you read, consider the following questions:

1. According to the author, how did the cartoons depict Muhammad?

Haroon Siddiqui, "Denmark Embroiled in Muslim Controversy," *Toronto Star*, February 2, 2006, p. A17. Copyright © 2006 Toronto Star Newspapers, Ltd. Reproduced by permission of Torstar Syndication Services.

2. What reason did Carsten Juste give for refusing to apologize for printing the cartoons, as reported by Haroon Siddiqui?

3. What double standard is at the heart of the conflict over the publication of anti-Islamic views, in the author's opinion?

The protracted, still-raging controversy over a Danish newspaper's caricature of the Prophet Muhammad is a case study of the West's troubled relations with Muslims.

It features the easy clichés of the age—freedom of speech vs. Islamic intolerance, and open democratic debate vs. politically correct cravenness [cowardice].

But what it has actually exposed is the European media's tendency to exploit anti-immigrant, particularly anti-Muslim, bigotry, as well as the Danes' readiness to bow to the gods of commerce.

The story begins last fall [2005] when an author complained he could not get an artist to illustrate a children's book about Muhammad's life, given Islam's prohibition against depicting the Prophet, lest it lead to idolatry.

Jyllands-Posten, the conservative mass circulation daily, asked 40 illustrators to defy the ban. On Sept. 30, it published a dozen of their drawings.

The Cartoons and Their Impact

One depicted the Prophet as a bearded terrorist, with bulging eyes and a bomb-shaped turban with a burning fuse. Another had him wielding a sword. Another showed him as a crazed, knife-wielding bedouin [desert nomad]. Another placed him at the gates of heaven telling suicide bombers "Stop. Stop. We have run out of virgins!"

The first to complain were Danish Muslims. They were ignored. Muslim ambassadors to Denmark asked to meet the prime minister. Anders Fogh Rasmussen refused.

Flemming Rose, the paper's cultural editor, said he had commissioned the cartoons to break the self-censorship he felt had descended on Europe since the 2004 murder of Dutch filmmaker Theo van Gogh by a Muslim (since convicted and sentenced to life imprisonment). Editor Carsten Juste said he saw no reason to apologize.

Prime Minister Rasmussen walked a fine line, denouncing "any expression that attempts to demonize groups on the basis of religion or ethnic background," but adding that "freedom of speech is not negotiable."

As protests spread worldwide, Editor Juste struck a disingenuous note. "We are sorry if Muslims have been offended."

On Jan. 10 [2006], the cartoons were reprinted in Norway in an evangelical Christian newspaper.

Protests continued. The Arab League and the 56-member Organization of the Islamic Conference [OIC] issued formal condemnations. . . . Saudi Arabia recalled its ambassador from Denmark. Libya closed its embassy.

A grassroots consumer boycott of Danish and Norwegian products spread from Saudi Arabia across the Arabian Gulf.

Arla Foods—the Danish dairy, which sells about $421 million (U.S.) a year in that region—said sales had come to a "standstill." Other Danish firms also reported lost sales and cancelled business meetings.

In Copenhagen, the Confederation of Danish Industries accused *Jyllands-Posten* of jeopardizing $1 billion of annual sales to the Middle East.

Editor Juste went back to being defiant. The paper "cannot and will not" apologize. "If we were to, we'd be letting down generations who have fought for freedom of speech. Do we have to give up this right to protect Danish export interests?"

Meanwhile, in Iraq (where Denmark has 530 troops), thousands protested. In the West Bank, Danish flags were burnt. A

Encouraging Hate-Mongering

Freedom of press is not absolute, and must be used responsibly by those who claim it. Those who appreciate the importance of free speech for maintaining free and open society must ensure that it is not used by bigots to insult, insinuate, and marginalize. Rather than expanding the critical space to talk about religion in general, and the integration of Islam to Danish society in particular, *Jyllands-Posten* has irresponsibly used free speech to encourage hate-mongering.

Louay M. Safi,
"Danish Cartoons: Free Press or Hate Speech?"
iViews.com, February 10, 2006. www.iviews.com.

militant Fatah [Palestinian political party] group demanded that all Danes and Swedes leave the region, apparently confusing Sweden for Norway.

Sweden, Norway and Denmark urged their citizens to avoid travel to the Middle East.

A Belated Apology

By Monday evening [January 30, 2006], *Jyllands-Posten* had caved. "The drawings are not against the Danish law but have indisputably offended many Muslims, for which we shall apologize."

Yesterday [February 1, 2006], a newspaper in France and another in Germany published the cartoons, citing freedom of the press.

But the issue goes well beyond the old debate over whether freedom of expression has limits. It does in countries like Canada, which have anti-hate laws. But regardless of the presence or absence of legislated limits, every society has its own notions of what is acceptable and what is not.

We can be certain that the editors publishing the Muhammad caricatures would not smear their pages with anti-Semitic graffiti. Or commission drawings maligning the Pope, by depicting him, say, in compromising sexual positions.

And had the editors opted to be that offensive, we can be equally certain that not too many people would have been rushing to their defence.

It is this double standard that's at the heart of the repeated conflicts between the West and the world of Islam over how far anti-Islamic provocateurs can go in baiting Muslims, repeatedly, knowing full well the depth of Muslim feelings about their most cherished beliefs.

Invoking freedom of speech or the need to puncture political correctness are no more than smokescreens to hide that larger, and uglier, truth.

The Danes have neither defended freedom of speech well nor upheld another sacred secular principle, mutual respect between peoples of all faiths.

In balancing these two competing rights in this troubled world at this time, thinking people and responsible public institutions should err on the side of advancing mutual understanding, not fanning more conflicts.

"We cannot apologize for our right to publish material, even offensive material."

The Press Should Not Self-Censor Anti-Islamic Views

Flemming Rose

The following viewpoint was written by Flemming Rose, the culture editor of the Danish newspaper Jyllands-Posten. *His newspaper stoked controversy in September 2005, when it published twelve cartoons depicting the Islamic prophet Muhammad. Rose explains that he decided to publish the cartoons in response to an increase in self-censorship among artists and writers who feared offending Muslims with their works. He insists that in a secular democratic society, the press must be free to express and publish divergent views of Islam even if some people are offended by them.*

As you read, consider the following questions:

1. What incident at London's Tate gallery does the author cite as an example of self-censorship?

Flemming Rose, "Why I Published Those Cartoons," *Washington Post*, February 19, 2006, p. B01. Copyright © The Washington Post, 2006. Reproduced by permission of the author.

2. How does Flemming Rose interpret the drawing of Muhammad with a bomb in his turban?

3. How does the author respond to the charge that his paper applies a double standard when choosing which cartoons to publish?

Childish. Irresponsible. Hate speech. A provocation just for the sake of provocation. A PR [public relations] stunt. Critics of 12 cartoons of the prophet Muhammad I decided to publish in the Danish newspaper *Jyllands-Posten* have not minced their words. They say that freedom of expression does not imply an endorsement of insulting people's religious feelings, and besides, they add, the media censor themselves every day. So, please do not teach us a lesson about limitless freedom of speech.

I agree that the freedom to publish things doesn't mean you publish everything. *Jyllands-Posten* would not publish pornographic images or graphic details of dead bodies; swear words rarely make it into our pages. So we are not fundamentalists in our support for freedom of expression.

But the cartoon story is different.

Increasing Self-Censorship

Those examples have to do with exercising restraint because of ethical standards and taste; call it editing. By contrast, I commissioned the cartoons in response to several incidents of self-censorship in Europe caused by widening fears and feelings of intimidation in dealing with issues related to Islam. And I still believe that this is a topic that we Europeans must confront, challenging moderate Muslims to speak out. The idea wasn't to provoke gratuitously—and we certainly didn't intend to trigger violent demonstrations throughout the Muslim world. Our goal was simply to push back self-imposed limits on expression that seemed to be closing in tighter.

At the end of September [2005], a Danish stand-up comedian said in an interview with *Jyllands-Posten* that he had no problem urinating on the Bible in front of a camera, but he dared not do the same thing with the Koran.

This was the culmination of a series of disturbing instances of self-censorship. Last September [2005], a Danish children's writer had trouble finding an illustrator for a book about the life of Muhammad. Three people turned down the job for fear of consequences. The person who finally accepted insisted on anonymity, which in my book is a form of self-censorship. European translators of a critical book about Islam also did not want their names to appear on the book cover beside the name of the author, a Somalia-born Dutch politician who has herself been in hiding.

Around the same time, the Tate gallery in London withdrew an installation by the avant-garde artist John Latham depicting the Koran, Bible and Talmud torn to pieces. The museum explained that it did not want to stir things up after the London bombings [a series of suicide bombings carried out by British Islamic extremists on July 7, 2005]. (A few months earlier, to avoid offending Muslims, a museum in Göteborg, Sweden, had removed a painting with a sexual motif and a quotation from the Koran.)

Finally, at the end of September [2005], Danish Prime Minister Anders Fogh Rasmussen met with a group of imams [Muslim religious leaders], one of whom called on the prime minister to interfere with the press in order to get more positive coverage of Islam.

A Legitimate News Story

So, over two weeks we witnessed a half-dozen cases of self-censorship, pitting freedom of speech against the fear of confronting issues about Islam. This was a legitimate news story to cover, and *Jyllands-Posten* decided to do it by adopting the well-known journalistic principle: Show, don't tell. I wrote to

Freedom Must Be Protected

A central premise of the American experiment are these words from the Declaration of Independence: "All men are created equal, that they are endowed by their Creator with certain unalienable Rights, that among these are Life, Liberty and the pursuit of Happiness." There are similar statements in the U.S. Constitution, British Common Law, the Napoleonic Code and the U.N. [United Nations] Declaration of Human Rights. As a result, hundreds of millions in the United States and around the world enjoy freedom of speech, freedom of assembly, freedom of religion and many other rights.

These liberties have been won through centuries of debate, conflict and bloodshed. Radical jihadists want to sacrifice all we have learned by returning to a primitive and intolerant world. While modern society invites such radicals to peacefully exercise their faith, we cannot and will not sacrifice our fundamental freedoms.

Peter Hoekstra,
"Islam and Free Speech,"
Wall Street Journal, *March 26, 2008.*

members of the association of Danish cartoonists asking them "to draw Muhammad as you see him." We certainly did not ask them to make fun of the Prophet. Twelve out of 25 active members responded.

We have a tradition of satire when dealing with the royal family and other public figures, and that was reflected in the cartoons. The cartoonists treated Islam the same way they treat Christianity, Buddhism, Hinduism and other religions. And by treating Muslims in Denmark as equals they made a point: We are integrating you into the Danish tradition of satire because you are part of our society, not strangers. The cartoons are including, rather than excluding, Muslims.

The cartoons do not in any way demonize or stereotype Muslims. In fact, they differ from one another both in the way they depict the Prophet and in whom they target. One cartoon makes fun of *Jyllands-Posten*, portraying its cultural editors as a bunch of reactionary provocateurs. Another suggests that the children's writer who could not find an illustrator for his book went public just to get cheap publicity. A third puts the head of the anti-immigration Danish People's Party in a lineup, as if she is a suspected criminal.

One cartoon—depicting the Prophet with a bomb in his turban—has drawn the harshest criticism. Angry voices claim the cartoon is saying that the Prophet is a terrorist or that every Muslim is a terrorist. I read it differently: Some individuals have taken the religion of Islam hostage by committing terrorist acts in the name of the Prophet. They are the ones who have given the religion a bad name. The cartoon also plays into the fairy tale about Aladdin and the orange that fell into his turban and made his fortune. This suggests that the bomb comes from the outside world and is not an inherent characteristic of the Prophet.

No Double Standard

On occasion, *Jyllands-Posten* has refused to print satirical cartoons of Jesus, but not because it applies a double standard. In fact, the same cartoonist who drew the image of Muhammad with a bomb in his turban drew a cartoon with Jesus on the cross having dollar notes in his eyes and another with the Star of David attached to a bomb fuse. There were, however, no embassy burnings or death threats when we published those.

Has *Jyllands-Posten* insulted and disrespected Islam? It certainly didn't intend to. But what does respect mean? When I visit a mosque, I show my respect by taking off my shoes. I follow the customs, just as I do in a church, synagogue or other holy place. But if a believer demands that I, as a nonbeliever, observe his taboos in the public domain, he is not asking for my respect, but for my submission. And that is incompatible with a secular democracy.

This is exactly why Karl Popper, in his seminal work *The Open Society and Its Enemies*, insisted that one should not be tolerant with the intolerant. Nowhere do so many religions coexist peacefully as in a democracy where freedom of expression is a fundamental right. In Saudi Arabia, you can get arrested for wearing a cross or having a Bible in your suitcase, while Muslims in secular Denmark can have their own mosques, cemeteries, schools, TV and radio stations. I acknowledge that some people have been offended by the publication of the cartoons, and *Jyllands-Posten* has apologized for that. But we cannot apologize for our right to publish material, even offensive material. You cannot edit a newspaper if you are paralyzed by worries about possible insult.

Periodical Bibliography

The following articles have been selected to supplement the diverse views presented in this chapter.

Ayaan Hirsi Ali "The Role of Journalism Today," American Enterprise Institute for Public Policy Research, June 19, 2007. www.aei.org.

L. Brent Bozell III "Tony Blankley's Untimely Cry," *Human Events*, January 28, 2009. www.humanevents.com.

Steven Groves "Why the U.S. Should Oppose 'Defamation of Religions' Resolutions at the United Nations," *Heritage Foundation Backgrounder*, November 10, 2008.

Nat Hentoff "A Free Speech Killer," *Washington Times*, February 2, 2009.

David Lazarus "Hey FCC, Let Parents Be the Net Censors," *Los Angeles Times*, December 3, 2008.

Seth Leibsohn "New Censors' *Obsession*," *National Review Online*, September 25, 2008. www.nationalreview.com.

New York Sun "Tie-Breaker," June 26, 2007.

Matthew Rothschild "Mainstream Media Culpability," *Progressive*, July 2008.

Arlen Specter and Joe Lieberman "Foreign Courts Take Aim at Our Free Speech," *Wall Street Journal*, July 14, 2008.

Robert Spencer "Battling Censorship," *Washington Times*, July 20, 2007.

George F. Will "A Setback for the Censors," *Washington Post*, June 28, 2007.

OPPOSING
VIEWPOINTS®
SERIES

CHAPTER 2

Should the Internet Be Censored?

Chapter Preface

Since the widespread use of the Internet in homes and businesses began in the mid to late 1990s, a struggle has ensued between advocates of the unfettered flow of information and proponents of regulations on Internet content. Some view the Web as a technological frontier in which freedom must be maintained. Others insist that restrictions on Internet text and images are needed to protect children from sexual predators and pornographic materials. In order to understand the current debate over Internet censorship, it is useful to know the history of attempts to regulate Internet content.

The first major attempt by U.S. Congress to control the Internet was the Communications Decency Act (CDA) of 1996. This law made it illegal to send or display content to minors that was "patently offensive . . . obscene . . . or indecent." Online civil liberties organizations such as the Electronic Frontier Foundation (EFF) strongly opposed the law on the grounds that banning indecent speech would lead to the censorship of non-pornographic content such as certain works of literature and medical information related to body parts and functions. After various legal challenges, the U.S. Supreme Court agreed that the CDA went too far in banning "patently offensive" or "indecent speech," thereby largely gutting the law.

The next attempt by Congress to regulate Internet speech was the Child Online Protection Act (COPA) of 1998. This law was intended to resolve the problems the courts identified with the CDA. It required commercial distributors of "material harmful to minors" to bar users under the age of 18 from accessing their sites. Like the CDA, COPA went through many legal challenges and counter-challenges. In the end, the courts found that the law's definition of *obscenity* was too broad and that COPA, therefore, violated the First Amendment right to free speech. In addition, the courts noted that a less restrictive means of protecting children from illicit content existed: Internet filtering software.

The third major attempt by Congress to regulate Internet content was the Children's Internet Protection Act (CIPA) of 2000. Unlike the CDA or COPA, CIPA did not target Internet providers. Instead, it required schools and libraries receiving certain government technology discounts to install Internet filtering software on their computers. Because the law included a provision allowing libraries to remove the blocking software at the request of an adult, it was deemed not to interfere with adults' First Amendment rights and was therefore upheld by the U.S. Supreme Court.

Congress has made additional attempts to regulate online content in recent years. In both 2006 and 2007, it debated but failed to pass the Deleting Online Predators Act (DOPA). This law would be similar to CIPA in that it would require schools and libraries receiving particular government technology discounts to block Internet content. In this case, however, it would require them to block access to specific social networking sites such as MySpace and Facebook. Supporters of the law argue that child predators use such sites in an attempt to gain access to children, while bullies use them to harass their peers. Critics of the proposed law contend that, just as with previous attempts to censor the Web, it would result in the blocking of legitimate educational content.

The legal issues surrounding regulation of Internet content are complex. While all concerned agree that it is important to keep children safe in an increasingly technological world, this goal must be balanced against the need to protect the First Amendment rights of all Americans. This tension between freedom and government regulation form the foundation of the debates in the following chapter on Internet censorship.

> *"Filtering software . . . can be close to*
> *100 percent effective at blocking porn."*

Internet Filters Are Effective

Jacob Sullum

In the following viewpoint, Jacob Sullum argues Internet filtering software can effectively prevent children from accessing pornography online. Because such software is increasingly effective, Sullum concludes, there is no need for heavy-handed government regulations that will impose costs on Internet companies and threaten the free speech rights of adults. Sullum is the senior editor of Reason *magazine and Reason.com, which are publications of the Reason Foundation, a libertarian think tank.*

As you read, consider the following questions:

1. As reported by the author, in what ways was the Child Online Protection Act (COPA) deemed too narrow and too broad by Judge Lowell Reed Jr.?

2. What were the penalties for violating COPA, according to Jacob Sullum?

3. According to the author, how can the problem of over-blocking be overcome?

Jacob Sullum, "Can Uncle Sam Save Your Innocence?" *Reason Online*, March 28, 2007. Copyright © 2007 by Creators Syndicate Inc. Reproduced by permission of the author.

Congress has been trying to stop kids from seeing online pornography since 1996. Its first attempt, the Communications Decency Act [CDA], was overturned by the Supreme Court, and its second attempt, the Child Online Protection Act (COPA), seems destined for the same fate. The Court already has upheld a preliminary injunction blocking enforcement of COPA, and last week [March 2007] a federal judge made the injunction permanent.[1]

For more than a decade, then, parents have stood by helplessly as their children have been bombarded by dirty pictures. Well, not exactly. As U.S. District Judge Lowell Reed Jr. noted when he issued his injunction, filtering software used by parents and Internet service providers is much more effective than COPA would have been at keeping porn away from kids (or perhaps I should say "keeping kids away from porn," which better describes the reality of the situation).

The insistence that there nevertheless ought to be a law, which could still be heard in the wake of Reed's decision, betrays a disregard for the damage done to freedom of speech by heavy-handed efforts to make the Internet safe for children. It also reflects a knee-jerk statism [centralized government control] that demands a top-down, one-size-fits-all solution even when diverse, decentralized responses clearly work better.

Too Narrow and Too Broad

Reed concluded that COPA is both too narrow and too broad. It is too narrow because it does not apply to Web sites based in foreign countries, which account for something like half of online pornography. It is too broad because it covers not just pornography but any discussion or depiction of sexuality deemed "harmful to minors"—i.e., anyone under 17.

The law thus could apply to material, such as sex education, that is inappropriate for 3-year-olds, even if it's OK for

1. On January 21, 2009, the U.S. Supreme Court refused to hear an appeal of the lower court's injunction, thereby effectively killing COPA.

Government Should Not Legislate Morality

Protecting minors is important. The government has a place in making sure they have adequate health care, opportunities for a good education and a safe living environment. But it has no place in legislating the morality of online media as viewed by children. Parents should be making responsible, informed decisions about their children's activity on the Internet, and there are filters available to assist them in controlling a minor's time online.

Will Harris,
"Judge Correct in Striking Down Online Porn Law,"
Daily Reveille, *March 26, 2007.*

16-year-olds, never mind adults. COPA prohibits "commercial" sites (those that sell content or ad space) from making such material available to minors, threatening violators with a six-month prison sentence and fines of up to $50,000 a day.

Web site operators can escape those penalties "by requiring use of a credit card, debit account, adult access code, or adult personal identification number" before allowing access to potentially objectionable text or pictures. Any such requirement would impose costs on Web sites, compromise readers' privacy, and deter adult visitors. How likely would you be to cough up a credit card number for the privilege of reading an article?

Given this reality, Web sites would have a strong incentive to steer clear of anything sex-related that might be considered inappropriate for children. Without a single prosecution, the law could have a substantial effect on material available to adults.

Worse, as Reed concluded based on expert testimony, none of the "age verification" options mentioned in COPA is a reliable way to verify age. The law thus would cost Web sites money, inconvenience adults, reduce readership, and chill on-line speech without accomplishing the avowed objective of shielding minors from pornography.

An Effective Alternative

Filtering software, by contrast, is easy and cheap (often free) to use, and it can be close to 100 percent effective at blocking porn, whether it originates in the United States or abroad. Even the worst-performing programs, Reed found, block around 90 percent of sexually explicit material.

While mistakenly preventing access to unobjectionable Web sites remains a problem, dynamic filtering using improved algorithms has reduced the frequency of overblocking to as low as 5 percent, and parents can always add erroneously blocked sites to the "white list" of approved addresses. Filters can be adjusted based on the age and maturity of the child (even for several different children) and the subjects parents consider inappropriate (e.g., sex, violence, drugs, racism). Passwords prevent kids from circumventing the controls.

This kind of flexibility is impossible to achieve through legislative diktat [decree]. Filters allow parents to choose the kind of protection that best suits their values and their children. Most important, unlike laws that threaten to impose preschool propriety on everyone, they can be turned off by grown-ups.

| "We can filter content all we want . . .
but at the end of the day, keeping students safe involves much, much more."

Internet Filters Are Ineffective

Matt Villano

*In the following viewpoint, writer Matt Villano argues that In-
ternet filters alone are not enough to protect children from online
pornography, predators, and harassment. While such programs
can play a role in keeping children safe, they have various flaws
that cause them to either block useful information or fail to
block harmful content. Due to these shortcomings, Villano contends, experts should implement prevention and education measures that will equip students with the knowledge they need to
avoid danger while online.*

As you read, consider the following questions:

1. What is wrong with the Children's Internet Protection
   Act (CIPA), as reported by the author?

2. What example does Matt Villano use to illustrate the
   problems caused by an overzealous use of filters?

Matt Villano, "What Are We Protecting Them From?" *T H E Journal (Technological Ho-
rizons in Education)*, vol. 35, no. 5, May 2008, pp. 48–52. Copyright © 2008 101 Communications Inc. Reproduced by permission.

3. What can Finland teach U.S. educators about how to protect children online, according to the author?

On June 23, 2003, in writing the Supreme Court's majority opinion that upheld the constitutionality of the Children's Internet Protection Act (CIPA), the late Chief Justice William Rehnquist shot down concerns that the law's mandated Internet filters would block users of public library computers from visiting unobjectionable Web sites. "Any such concerns are dispelled by the ease with which patrons may have the filtering software disabled," Rehnquist wrote. "When a patron encounters a blocked site, he need only ask a librarian to unblock it."

The ease with which patrons may have the filtering software disabled.

Oh really?

In a debate that has so much to do with the fine lines of meaning and interpretation, this assumption, according to on-line safety expert Nancy Willard, is what's all wrong with CIPA, which requires any school or library receiving funding from the federal E-Rate program [which provides institutions with telecommunication services and Internet access at discounted rates] to deploy Web filtering technology that prevents users from viewing objectionable material while they are using the institution's computers. Willard, director of the Center for Safe and Responsible Internet Use in Eugene, OR, argues that Web filters actually can threaten, not protect, students' security.

"Say there's a report of material that is posted on MySpace that relates to student safety or well-being, and that information is reported to a counselor," she explains, "the counselor needs to immediately get past the filter to review the material. Otherwise you have the potential for violence or suicide. In many schools, the ability to rapidly override the filter has not been established, which is impairing instructional activities as well as jeopardizing student safety."

Are Filters Best?

It's only one of many points of contention Willard and other educators have raised in opposition to CIPA since its enactment in 2000, as well as the various similar pieces of federal and state legislation that have since been introduced in the effort to protect children from online predators and offensive Web content while in public schools and libraries. No one disputes the need to protect kids from the harm that lurks online. What's at issue is whether or not mandated Internet filters are the best way to achieve those safeguards—or whether the filters aren't up to the task and are actually interfering with the educational mission by obstructing use of important Web 2.0 tools.[1]

The benefits of the legislation are apparent. On the most basic level, some degree of mandatory filtering is certainly better than no filtering, which leaves school networks completely open for students to visit whatever Web sites they wish. With the new filters, access to pornographic Web sites, gambling sites, and other popular distractions is almost entirely locked down.

"Under the old system, where districts were left to handle these things on their own, many schools were opening the door to just about everything," says Jayne Moore, director of instructional technology and school library media for the Maryland Department of Education. "At least with a filter, districts have a good sense of control over what their kids are doing on the Internet when they're at school."

Problems with Filters

Still, CIPA's implementation has faced many issues, the first being its irrelevance. By the time the bill was passed into law,

---

1. Web 2.0 is the second generation of the Web, which includes more interactive components, such as file-sharing, video-sharing, and social-networking sites.

many school districts had already purchased content filters with scanning technology that far exceeded the requirements set forth by the federal government.

A second issue is sheer overzealousness. In many cases, schools have cranked up their filters so high that students searching for an innocuous but easily misunderstood term can't get anywhere. David Burt, who runs the blog Filtering Facts, which is dedicated to providing the newest information and research about Internet filtering, tells the familiar story about students who were searching for information about breast cancer, but were impeded because their search contained the word breast.

"When they are turned up to the highest settings, many of these filters actually block good information, too," says Burt, who works as a product manager at Microsoft. "For teachers who rely on the Internet to help with specific lessons, this can become very frustrating, to say the least."

Perhaps the biggest problem with CIPA-inspired filtering has become proxy servers. These servers, so-called "safe" sites that act as proxies and forward Web page requests to other servers, enable students to dupe district filters into thinking they are visiting one site when they are in fact visiting something very different—and usually forbidden.

Willard says proxy servers are more of a problem than district administrators even know. She recounts a recent visit to a school district during which she met with a handful of students as a focus group to find out what kind of safety issues concerned them. During a break in the action, Willard asked them if they knew how to get around the district's Internet filters.

Across the board, the students said yes.

"Schools across this country are spending millions and millions of dollars for technical solutions to comply with CIPA," Willard says, "but our students can easily get around just about everything we throw at them." . . .

An Ounce of Prevention

Opponents of Web filtering legislation argue it is simply the wrong way to approach online safety. "We can filter content all we want," says Jim Culbert, information security analyst at Duval County Public Schools in Jacksonville, FL, "but at the end of the day, keeping students safe involves much, much more."

If filters are well-intentioned but inadequate, how do we address the real need to protect students from online harassment?

According to Willard, commonsense methods can do more than legislation. "We should tell kids that if something that looks 'yucky' comes up on the screen, turn off the monitor and tell an adult," she says. "That essential safety technique is not being taught because of the misplaced reliance on filters."

Education Efforts

Many K-12 technology experts say the best solution long-term is shifting the emphasis from policing the way students use the Internet to educating them about using it more safely. In Virginia, for instance, a law passed last year [2007] prescribes an Internet safety curriculum in every public school. Now every Virginia schoolchild must be taught about the dangers of interacting on the Web, starting in kindergarten.

In 2007, Rep. Brad Ellsworth (D-IN) took this thinking to the national stage, proposing HR 3871, the e-Keep the Internet Decent and Safe (e-KIDS) Act, which would mandate that schools educate minors about appropriate online behavior. Other laws under consideration in Congress right now would provide up to $5 million a year to fund i-SAFE, a nonprofit foundation in Carlsbad, CA, whose mission is to educate and empower youth to make their Internet experiences safe and responsible.

Don Knezek, CEO of the International Society for Technology in Education in Washington, D.C., says his group is putting together professional development courses to help teachers develop techniques for educating their students about responsible Internet use. As part of the program, teachers will be encouraged to spend time in online communities to get a sense of how social networking sites work, and what kind of "buddies" students are liable to meet there. "Abstinence from technology is a losing battle," Knezek says. "To not teach technology use responsibly is neglecting the charge of universal education."

Over time, these kinds of efforts could yield huge dividends—they have worked elsewhere. Julie Walker, executive director of the American Association of School Librarians in Chicago, recently traveled to Finland, where educators have taught students about responsible Internet use for years. Walker says most Finnish schools don't even have filters—at least not the kind any technologist would need to worry about.

"Over there, thanks to solid teaching, the filters are in the students' heads," she says. "Students come into school with a sense of responsibility for their learning and a sense of why they're there. Ultimately, that's where we need to be too."

> "Net neutrality regulation would strip away the ability of broadband providers to stop child pornography, obscenity, and other dangerous content on the Web from reaching our children."

Laws to Make the Internet Neutral Will Endanger Families

Cesar Conda

Many lawmakers and technology experts advocate laws that would prevent Internet service providers from controlling the content transmitted through their cables. Proponents insist that such laws, commonly referred to as "net neutrality laws," are necessary to protect freedom of speech. In the following viewpoint, Cesar Conda rejects these claims. He contends that net neutrality laws would impose costly burdens on the telecommunications industry, thereby impeding the growth of Internet technology. Moreover, they would prevent Internet service providers from blocking content that is harmful to children and families. Conda is a founding principal of Navigators Global, a government relations and strategic communications firm.

Cesar Conda, "Net Neutrality Regulation Hurts Families," Townhall.com, March 12, 2008. Reproduced by permission of the author.

As you read, consider the following questions:

1. What percentage of adults have a broadband Internet connection at home, according to the statistics cited by the author?

2. What examples does Cesar Conda cite to support his contention that the Internet is increasingly important to Americans?

3. What groups and individuals join Conda in opposing net neutrality laws, as reported by the author?

The Christian Coalition of America is an important voice for pro-family values. However, in recent testimony before the House Judiciary Committee, the group threw its support behind a new "Washington-knows-best" regulatory scheme that would not only stifle innovation and growth, but also limit the ability of America's parents to protect their children from objectionable and dangerous Internet content.

A Broadband Revolution

Today's Internet is an exciting and ever-evolving engine of phenomenal technological growth for our digital economy. The Internet also knows no political boundaries. Democrats and Republicans alike have identified high-speed Internet deployment, affordability and accessibility—for Americans from across all social backgrounds, in both rural and urban areas—as an important policy goal that all can agree upon.

According to the Pew Internet & American Life Project [a survey of Internet use by the Pew Research Center], 47 percent of adults have a broadband connection at home, a 17 percent increase in the last two years. This increase in broadband connections is transforming the way Americans communicate, learn and live their daily lives.

As recently as 2005, most Internet users were not watching streaming video or downloading television programs because

Technology Ownership by Household Type

	All adults (n = 2,252)	Married with child/ children (n = 482)	Other household types (n = 1770)	Other multi-member households (n = 1189)
Computer(s) in household	77%	93%	71%	81%
At least one household member goes online	77%	94%	71%	83%
Have a home broadband connection	52%	66%	47%	55%

TAKEN FROM: Pew Internet & American Life Project Networked Family Survey, December 13, 2007–January 13, 2008.

of bandwidth limitations (one hour of television viewing takes up 17,000 times more bandwidth than viewing a normal Web page). Today, students are more dependent on the Internet than ever before, as many classes and lessons are available through streaming video. At-risk patients can upload test results over a broadband connection, and doctors can share medical images with rural or homebound patients. New video technology allows American small business entrepreneurs to dive into the global market.

For the most part, Washington has kept the Internet free of burdensome regulation. This has allowed Internet service providers to invest in their broadband networks, thereby making them faster, smarter, and safer.

The Threat of "Net Neutrality"

But this broadband revolution could soon come to an end. Congressman Edward Markey (D-Massachusetts) has introduced legislation (misleadingly named the "Internet Freedom

Preservation Act") that would lead to so-called "network neutrality" regulation. Specifically, the Markey bill would "express the policy of the United States to safeguard . . . the Internet by adopting and enforcing baseline protections to guard against unreasonable discriminatory favoritism." In effect, the Markey bill establishes as policy that the Federal Communications Commission (FCC) will for the first time regulate the Internet. [Editor's note: The Markey bill died in committee.]

Such net neutrality legislation would not only kill the deployment of broadband connections, but would prohibit Internet service providers from managing their networks, which brings us back to the Christian Coalition of America, the newest member of the pro-net neutrality forces. During the hearing, the Christian Coalition accused broadband providers of China-like tactics to censor speech over the Internet. However, the fact is that the FCC already has rules prohibiting the blocking or delaying of e-mail or text messages.

More importantly, net neutrality regulation would strip away the ability of broadband providers to stop child pornography, obscenity, and other dangerous content on the Web from reaching our children. Parents are demanding family-friendly Internet filters and other controls to protect their children. Without effective controls available to families, schools, libraries and anywhere else children can access Internet content, it would take only one wrong click or one curious search to reach pornography, information on drugs, violent content or even child predators.

In a letter to members of Congress, a group of prominent social and economic conservatives, including Gary Bauer of American Values, David Keene of the American Conservative Union, Larry Cirignano of CatholicVote.org and Grover Norquist of Americans for Tax Reform, wrote: "It is critically important for parents and broadband service providers to continue to have these tools available to them because despite what network neutrality proponents may say, all content on the Web is not equal and should not be treated equally."

One of the most serious consequences of net neutrality is the subtle but frightening erosion of a parent's ability to safeguard their child's experience on the Internet. Rather than improving Internet service, net neutrality regulation would hurt our economy and our families.

| "The failure to enact strong net neutral-
ity legislation would mean an Internet
with gatekeepers."

Laws to Make the Internet Neutral Will Prevent Censorship

Damian Kulash

Damian Kulash is the lead singer and guitarist for the rock band OK Go. In the following viewpoint, he advocates the passage of "net neutrality" legislation, which would prevent Internet service providers from controlling the content that passes through their networks. Kulash insists that net neutrality laws will protect the rights of artists to create, distribute, and profit from their work and will ensure the right to free speech for all citizens.

As you read, consider the following questions:

1. What unethical behavior resulted from the pre-Internet music distribution system, according to Damian Kulash?

Damian Kulash, "Testimony on Net Neutrality and Free Speech on the Internet," *Hearing Before the Task Force on Competition Policy and Antitrust Laws of the Committee on the Judiciary*, House of Representatives, March 11, 2008. Reproduced by permission of the author.

2. By what percentage did OK Go's album sales increase after their treadmill video went online, as reported by the author?

3. What other businesses does the author cite to support his argument that the Internet must remain neutral?

My name is Damian Kulash; my band is called OK Go. We've been around for nearly 10 years, during which time we've sold over a half a million records, won a Grammy, played over 1,200 shows in 45 states and on 5 continents, and most important to us here today, had the good fortune to be one of the first bands to become truly successful via the Internet, where we've had tens of millions—maybe hundreds of millions—of streams, downloads, and Web site hits. We are among the tiny percentage of the world's musicians lucky enough to earn a living doing what we love, and we owe our livelihood in large part to our online success, a type of success that couldn't have been imagined just a decade ago. I'm here to ask you to protect the principles that have made the Internet great, and that have made it a place where a band like mine can succeed.

Mr. Chairman, the music business is experiencing a profound transformation right now—one that could mean either the dawn of a new era for American art and commerce, or its continued consolidation, coming at the expense of not just artists and musicians, but all Americans.

A Formidable Task

Since the dawn of recorded music early last century, the industry that emerged around it has been based on the natural bottleneck that existed between musicians and the music listening public. Musicians needed a way to reach all those people, and people needed a way to get all that music, and a complicated and profitable system emerged to connect the dots.

The mechanics of making and distributing records were formidable: professional recording studios were expensive to maintain and operate, manufacturing and packaging records was costly and complicated, and getting those records onto the turntables of America required a vast and complex network of warehouses, shippers, distributors, and retailers.

On top of that there was the question of exposing and promoting music to the public. Commercial radio has long been the only medium for reaching most people, and a handful of radio programmers effectively choose what music the country would hear. Naturally, there is intense and expensive competition for their attention. Later came MTV, where once again a few people pick a few songs for the whole country.

As I'm sure you're well aware, the extreme bottlenecks of this system encouraged pretty ethically challenged behavior at times. Some songs succeeded primarily on the merits of the drugs and Super Bowl tickets that were delivered to radio stations with them. But I'm not here today to question or condemn how business was done, but rather to simply recognize that the architecture of the industry, the system of powerful gatekeepers, had a profound influence on what music got made and listened to in America, and under what conditions. Gatekeepers, of course, sometimes used their power to compel artists to enter onerous contracts.

Removing the Bottlenecks

Today, that system has been turned on its head. Digital technologies have begun to remove the bottlenecks, and the industry founded on them faces a crisis, even as music itself enters a new golden age. Making, distributing, and listening to music is easier now than ever before. Anyone with access to a decent computer now has recording tools that the professionals of my parents' generation couldn't have dreamt of—making high quality recordings is now nearly as easy as word processing. With a few clicks of a mouse, recordings can be distributed to pretty much any place on the globe, and listened to practically anywhere. If you've been on the Metro [subway] recently, you've no doubt noticed that the entire commuting community has headphones on—they're all listening to digital music players. I'd bet that more music is being listened to now than ever before in history. Musical ideas are spreading and combining and growing, even as the rigid structure of the traditional music business is crumbling. All sorts of exciting new things are possible. It's an exhilarating time.

It certainly has been for my band. Let me give you a quick overview of how we got where we are. OK Go started in 1999 and followed a pretty well-worn path for the first few years. We developed a following at local clubs in our hometown of Chicago, spent as much time on the road as we could afford to, eventually landed ourselves a record deal with a major label, and then played the promotional game as it is generally played in the majors: a ton of no-profit touring, a lot of free shows for radio stations, as many interviews as we could get, and the occasional music video, where the cost is advanced by our label and deducted from our royalties. Our first record, which came out in 2002, did decently well: on the modern rock radio charts we just barely broke into the top 20, and on *Billboard*'s sales charts we made it to about 100. We were in the middle of the pack: successful enough to keep going, but straggling for every fan we could find.

Do-It-Yourself

In 2005 we released a second album and that's when our story takes a turn pertinent to the subject at hand today. When the record came out, we did all the standard promotion that our label advised, but we also decided to launch our own online campaign with simple, absurd videos we made ourselves.

With the help of my sister, we choreographed a parodic dance routine and shot a single-take home video of us performing it in my backyard. If you include the Starbucks run, the total budget for the video was about $20. We posted the clip online, and it caught on like wildfire. We watched, astonished, as the video racked up hundreds of thousands, then millions, then tens of millions of hits at online video sites. Before long, we were getting offers to play to thousands in countries where our record had never even been released.

And something even wilder started happening: fans started posting their own versions of the video. Thrilled by the direct connection with our fans, we launched a dance contest, and received homemade remakes of our video from all over the world. We got hundreds of entries, videos of the dance at weddings, in churches, at high school talent shows, in firehouses, and even a version performed by animated LEGOs. This is a whole new phenomenon, a feedback loop of creativity that allows us to be more than just a commercial product to our fans—we are the center of an active, creative community.

We followed that video up with another that we shot at my sister's home in Orlando. It was a single take again, and we were dancing again, but this time on eight moving treadmills. To my knowledge, this routine has only been repeated four times (once in Japan, once in Mexico, and twice in the United States), and for the record, we assume no liability for those dumb enough to try it. In the first two days after we posted the clip on YouTube, it was viewed a million times. In the month after it went online, our album sales increased nearly 4,000%. We won a Grammy for the video, beating out much bigger acts with exponentially bigger budgets and promotional campaigns. Now we get stopped in Times Square by people old enough to be our grandparents. To date, it's been viewed over 30 million times on YouTube alone.

The Importance of the Internet

Whether you think our videos are brilliant or gimmicky—I'd be the first to say they're a little of both—they've done more to promote our music to an audience around the world than anything else we or our label has produced. For seven years we barely covered our bills, and since our Internet success, we've become a very successful operation. We believe the videos were so loved because they came directly from us. There was no one telling us what we could or couldn't do, no middlemen or marketers, and we didn't have to sell a committee of gatekeepers on our idea before we could take it to our fans. Our success couldn't have happened in the pay-to-play music industry of ten years ago, or in a world without an open, unbiased, and unfettered Internet.

Of course, like most bands, we use the Internet for everything today; it's not just a medium for our videos. We connect with fans through our Web site, our online forums, and through social networking sites like MySpace and Facebook. We alert our online fans to concerts and television and radio appearances, and we promote those appearances to new fans. We sell our merchandise and CDs and book our tours online. We broadcast some concerts online, and have done many performances solely for an online audience. Today, as I speak to you, some dedicated portion of our fans is listening to this testimony, online. (Hi guys). Basically, the Internet stops just short of writing our music for us, but it takes care of just about everything else.

Net Neutrality Is Crucial

This part of our story is common to every band working today. We've joined with over eight hundred other bands in the Future of Music Coalition's "Rock the Net" campaign, and each of them—and I'd venture to say pretty much every working musician out there today—will tell you how vital an open and neutral Internet is to their business.

Mr. Chairman, let me be very clear here, though: With the big opportunities and big changes that digital technologies have brought to the music world, there are great unknowns

Diverse Voices and Alternative Views

This is what the net neutrality debate is really about, at its core: The ability of diverse voices and alternative views to continue to be heard, whether or not it is profitable for Viacom or Disney to air these views. It's about the ability of conservative activists and candidates to communicate directly to our members and supporters without paying an additional toll to Verizon or AT&T.

Jim Backlin,
"The Conservative Argument FOR Net Neutrality,"
Christian Coalition of America,
September 14, 2007. www.cc.org.

for musicians. My peers and I run small businesses, and like all entrepreneurs, we want to ensure that our work is valued, that we can earn livings, and that our good ideas can make us good money. I am no fan of piracy. You will not find a songwriter or musician out there who doesn't want to get paid, but piracy issues must be addressed by innovations that build on an open Internet, not shut it down.

We believe people are willing to pay for good music in their lives. That hasn't changed, and the smart folk who build new systems capitalizing on the strengths of the Internet will reap big rewards. Net neutrality is necessary for the growth of new businesses and business models, and creating a new legitimate digital music business is critical to artists and the music industry. To put it simply, without net neutrality, I would not be sitting here today. If companies think they are going to protect their profits by erecting artificial bottlenecks, artists and their fans will lose. The new system that's emerging in the music world cannot return to a gatekeeper system—a system where the success of our ideas was determined solely by the middlemen who delivered them.

Keep the Internet Free

This principle extends beyond the realm of music, it applies to everything on the Internet: We cannot allow a system of gatekeepers to be built into the network as a whole. We must protect the basic equality that has made the Internet so great, and make sure the few existing broadband providers can't use their market power to erect new bottlenecks for music or any other industry. The failure to enact strong net neutrality legislation would mean an Internet with gatekeepers; an Internet that exists for the profit of a few, rather than the good of the many; a society where value comes not from the quality of information, but from the control of access to it.

Creativity and innovation are the lifeblood of any successful endeavor, whether artistic, commercial, or political. There are only two guitar companies who make the majority of guitars sold in America, but luckily they don't control what we play on those guitars. Whether we use Macs or PCs doesn't govern what our minds can bring to life with our computers. The telephone company doesn't get to decide what we discuss over our phone lines. Similarly, the companies who deal with the nuts and bolts of the Internet should not determine what we can do, or make, or access, or dream up while we're using it. The Internet has always been a place for freedom of speech, art, and commerce. We should keep it that way.

Until now, the Internet has fostered an explosion of creativity, innovation, and progress not in spite of its level playing field—but precisely *because* it is a level playing field. It's as close to a genuine meritocracy as we've ever seen. It's a place where my band's $20 video found a wider audience than the industry's million-dollar productions, because ours was simply better. Legislation to protect this level playing field is essential not just for the music community, but for all of us. The world of tomorrow must be built on our society's best ideas, not just those ideas that align with interests of a few powerful gate-keepers.

We'll do our part. We'll keep making the best songs, the best videos, and the best ideas we can. And on behalf of millions of Americans, musicians and artists, both aspiring and established, I am asking today that Congress do its part, too. Make sure there is always a fertile place for all our good ideas to flourish. Do not allow the few existing broadband providers to build new bottlenecks. Enshrine the Internet's level playing field in law.

> *"The greatest danger of network neutrality may be the outright censorship of speech that it promises."*

Laws to Make the Internet Neutral May Cause Censorship

Phil Kerpen

In the following viewpoint, Phil Kerpen opposes the passage of "net neutrality" laws, which would prevent Internet service providers from controlling the content they make available to users. Kerpen insists that such laws would lead to decreased private investment in Internet technology and would therefore impede development of the Web. Even worse, he contends, net neutrality laws would allow the government to censor speech on the Internet. Kerpen is director of policy for Americans for Prosperity, a conservative public policy advocacy organization, and chairman of the Internet Freedom Coalition, a group that oppose government regulation of the Internet.

Phil Kerpen, "Next Up for Nationalization: The Internet," *National Review Online*, November 13, 2008. Copyright © 2008 by National Review, Inc., 215 Lexington Avenue, New York, NY 10016. Reproduced by permission.

As you read, consider the following questions:

1. What example of a "bandwidth hog" does the author cite?

2. What is the problem with large-scale infrastructure management by the government, according to Phil Kerpen?

3. What example of censorship of speech does the author cite to illustrate the potential consequences of net neutrality?

Following the nationalization of investment banks, Fannie and Freddie,[1] consumer banks, and private insurance companies, taxpayers are likely asking: What's left for the federal government to nationalize?

How about the Internet?

Network neutrality, or net neutrality, is the beneficent-sounding name for sweeping new government regulatory power that would prohibit Internet service providers from innovating in their own networks. This could lead to much less broadband investment by private companies, and could potentially force government subsidization, control, and outright nationalization of the Internet. The implications of this are chilling.

Big Problems

President-elect [Barack] Obama and most congressional Democrats—under pressure from groups like Free Press, MoveOn.org, and corporate heavyweight Google—favor a

1. "Fannie" refers to the Federal National Mortgage Association commonly known as Fannie Mae. "Freddie" refers to the Federal Home Loan Mortgage Corporation commonly known as Freddie Mac. The federal government took control of both institutions in September 2008.

A Threat to Free Speech

"Net neutrality" has a pleasing ring. But government mandates requiring broadband ISPs [Internet service providers] to make available their networks for carrying or posting content they might prefer not to carry or post implicates ISPs' free speech rights. Under traditional First Amendment jurisprudence, it is as much a free speech infringement to compel a speaker to convey messages against the speaker's wishes as it is to prevent a speaker from conveying messages.

Randolph J. May,
"Communications Policy Pirouettes,"
Washington Times, *January 21, 2007.*

network-neutrality regime. In its strictest form, such a regime would require every bit that travels over a network to be treated the same way. That might sound fair in theory, but it means big problems in practice. If broadband providers can't manage their network traffic, they can't offer high-quality, high-value services that are free from the degradation of bandwidth hogs—like teenagers who download huge amounts of bootleg movies, music, and games from file-sharing networks.

Robert Kahn and David Farber, the technologists known respectively as the father and grandfather of the Internet, have been highly critical of network-neutrality mandates. Kahn has pointed out that to incentivize innovation, network operators must be allowed to develop new technologies within their own networks first—something that network-neutrality mandates could prevent. Farber has urged Congress not to enact net-neutrality mandates that would prevent significant improvements to the Internet.

Less Private Investment, More Government

Without the flexibility to develop technologies that can most efficiently serve customers while generating revenue, there will be less private investment in upgrading the capacity of the Internet. Larry Lessig of Stanford, a leading proponent of net neutrality, says openly that it will lead to less private investment in the Internet and therefore will require the government to step in with the investment of tax dollars. Lessig's rationale is that "Broadband is infrastructure—like highways, if not railroads."

Vint Cerf, Google's chief net-neutrality propagandist, agrees. Cerf calls for the effective nationalization of the Internet, arguing that "incentives could be provided that would render the Internet more like the public road system ... not owned by the private sector," with its use "essentially open to all."

Not only does the Internet in its current form work much better, and improve much more quickly, than government-run highways and railroads, but anyone who knows anything about highway and railroad contracts knows that large-scale infrastructure management by the government invites politically motivated deal-making as well as rampant fraud and abuse.

The Threat of Censorship

Yet the greatest danger of network neutrality may be the outright censorship of speech that it promises. Here's an example: University of Sunderland professor Alex Lockwood says nationalization of the Internet is one way to get a handle on the problem, in his view, of scientists skeptical of global warming who use the Internet to disseminate their research. His reasoning shows how easily the rationale for regulation can creep from network structure to content control:

> I would argue that climate disinformation online is a form
> of cultural and political malware every bit as threatening to

our new media freedoms, used not to foster a forum for open politics but to create, in Nancy Fraser's term, a "multiplicity of fragmented publics" that harms not only our democracy, but our planet.

Just like that, the American ideal of pluralism is dismissed as fragmentation, while free speech gives way to political correctness. Whatever you think about the global warming debate, a similar case can be constructed for any controversial issue, making a government-run or government-controlled Internet subject to political manipulation that, even if well-intentioned, would serve to shut down our greatest forum for free speech.

Supporters of network neutrality won't admit to any of this. In fact, they'll tell you the opposite—that network neutrality will preserve your freedoms. In an ironic twist, one of the scare tactics they use is the idea that phone and cable companies may start blocking access to political Web sites. Of course, this is exceedingly unlikely in a competitive marketplace where customers can take their business elsewhere. But it is very possible in a world of government monopoly.

It all starts with the nice-sounding slogan: network neutrality. Buyer beware.

Periodical Bibliography

The following articles have been selected to supplement the diverse views presented in this chapter.

Ernie Allen	"In Child Pornography, Fight Harder," *Christian Science Monitor*, November 26, 2007.
Dick Armey	"Spare the Net," *Washington Times*, April 22, 2008.
Mary Ann Bell	"The Elephant in the Room: School Districts Nationwide Are Voluntarily Filtering the Filters—And No One Is Talking About It," *School Library Journal*, January 2007.
Mona Charen	"Look Who's Censoring Now," Townhall.com, June 13, 2008. www.townhall.com.
Harry Lewis	"Not Your Father's Censorship," *Chronicle of Higher Education*, January 16, 2009.
Maclean's	"Plug the Porn Pipeline," June 18, 2008.
Tom Plate	"Cutting Down on the Lust, Raising the Caution Flag," *San Diego Business Journal*, January 7, 2008.
Register-Guard	"Censoring the Internet," July 2, 2008. www.registerguard.com.
Leslie Scrivener	"Generation XXX: Sex and the Teenage Brain," *Toronto Star*, January 17, 2009.
David Weinberger	"Beyond Net Neutrality," *Boston Globe*, February 23, 2008.

OPPOSING
VIEWPOINTS®
SERIES

CHAPTER 3

Is Free Speech Censored Worldwide?

Chapter Preface

On June 8, 2009, the government of North Korea sentenced American journalists Laura Ling and Euna Lee to twelve years of hard labor for "committing hostilities against the Korean nation and illegal entry." The reporters, who worked for Current TV, a media company cofounded by former vice president Al Gore, had been working on a story about North Korean refugees when they were detained in the border region between North Korea and China. While North Korea's government accused the women of "committing hostilities," their families insisted they were merely gathering news and had not intended to enter North Korean territory.

Reporters Without Borders (RWB), an international organization that works to increase press freedom around the world, strongly condemned the detention and punishment of the journalists. "These twelve-year sentences are a terrible shock," the organization said on its Web site. "The authorities in Pyongyang [the capital of North Korea] must urgently reverse this decision and allow Ling and Lee to rejoin their families." The goal of the punishment, according to Reporters Without Borders, was to frighten other journalists and discourage them from reporting on the region. Indeed, in RWB's 2008 "Worldwide Press Freedom Index," a ranking of all the nations of the world on the basis of press freedom, North Korea is second from the bottom.

North Korea is not the only country guilty of suppressing freedom of the press, according to Reporters Without Borders. In its 2008 annual index, the organization identified various countries as dangerous "black zones" for the press, including Iraq, Pakistan, Afghanistan, and Somalia. In these places, due to ongoing war or political unrest, journalists face the threat of kidnapping, murder, and arbitrary arrest on a daily basis. Even lower on the list are nations ruled by dictators, authoritarian monarchies, or other repressive forms of government, where journalists are subjected to police and judicial harassment. These countries dot the corners of the world—China and Vietnam in Asia; Iran in Central Asia; Zimbabwe, Congo, and Eritrea (the only country in the world below North Korea on the index) in Africa; and Libya, Syria, and Saudi Arabia in the Middle East. Censorship of the Internet is on the rise as well, according to Reporters Without Borders. While China still leads the "Internet black hole" ranking, the organization reports, Syria and Egypt are also employing Internet surveillance and blocking technology to silence journalists.

It may be unfair to hold all nations to the same free speech standards as those of Western democracies. Not all cultures value personal freedom as highly as Western cultures, and not all forms of government encode the right to free speech in their constitutions. However, most in the West believe that everyone deserves the right to express their opinions and receive information about the conduct of their government. At the very least, journalists and citizens should not be punished, harassed, or intimidated for merely gathering and conveying information. This belief underlies the viewpoints in the following chapter on the status of free speech worldwide.

> *"The idea is not just to stop people from finding 'dangerous' material online. It's to create an atmosphere in which none seek it."*

The Internet Is Censored in Repressive Countries

Adam B. Kushner

In the following viewpoint, Adam B. Kushner, a senior writer for Newsweek, *argues that repressive governments around the world are using increasingly invasive techniques to prevent their citizens from accessing or transmitting information freely via the Internet. China, Vietnam, Saudi Arabia, Egypt, and other countries routinely block Web sites, according to Kushner. More ominously, they are using terror tactics, such as creating an atmosphere of constant surveillance, to prevent citizens from actively seeking out or sharing information that is critical of the government.*

As you read, consider the following questions:

1. How does the author define "repression 2.0"?

Adam B. Kushner, "Repression 2.0," *Newsweek*, April 14, 2008. Copyright © 2008 Newsweek, Inc. All rights reserved. Reproduced by permission.

2. What is the crudest Internet censorship tool being used by repressive governments, according to Adam B. Kushner?

3. How does the case of Egyptian blogger Wael Abbas illustrate the new form of censorship in repressive countries, as described by the author?

In the latest twist on Internet repression, governments don't just censor, they scare. Last week [April 2008], for example, the Chinese government broadcast a text message to cell phone users in Lhasa, Tibet, where Beijing has cracked down on protests in recent weeks. The message demanded that users "obey the law" and "follow the rules," and no protester could have mistaken the meaning, or the messenger. If the government also managed to terrify even quiet, apolitical citizens, Chinese and Tibetan—well, so be it. Repression 2.0 is not a precise technology.

The essence of the new repression is a form of surveillance in which the spies make their presence known in order to seem like they are everywhere. This strategy has emerged in recent years as authoritarian governments, led by China, have realized there are too many people online to control. State censors can't keep eyes on the 210 million Internet users in China, the 18 million in Iran, nor the 6 million in Egypt. The idea is not just to stop people from finding "dangerous" material online. It's to create an atmosphere in which none will seek it.

From Censorship to Surveillance

Repression 1.0 was simpler, but less effective. There, the idea was outright censorship, and it still goes on today. As Internet users began communicating directly with individual Web sites, governments built (or bought) software filters designed to block any site they feared. Saudi Arabia blocks porn sites,

Vietnam blocks political sites and so on. It's just that the filters have never worked well. They blocked either too much content or too little. Just as with your family computer's anti-porn software, the high setting might filter informative sites about breast cancer. The low setting can filter known offenders, but it remains vulnerable to sites offering new content and new ways to evade filtration.

When Web 2.0 technologies—like Web mail and social networking sites—began to take off in 2002, they made it harder for censors to know what to block. Some Facebook users might fill their profiles with criticism of the government, but others might credulously purvey official propaganda. Facebook could hurt the government or help it, depending on the user rather than on the site itself. So instead of stopping Netizens from reaching Web 2.0 sites like Facebook or Gmail, the authorities turned to surveillance.

Of course, surveillance itself doesn't curtail free expression. But unlike Stasi agents [East German secret police during the Communist era] listening through carefully hidden microphones, Web 2.0 spies don't hide.

Their crudest tool is compulsory registration—to blog, to secure an Internet connection or even to get a terminal at the neighborhood Internet café. While Internet cafés worldwide opened without much state interference in the late '90s, before long every government that limits speech also required Internet café goers to register with proprietors and to log in with government IDs. According to Ethan Zuckerman, a fellow at Harvard University's Berkman Center for Internet and Society, some nations like Zimbabwe even deploy security agents—or people who act like them—to wander the aisles at cafés, glancing at screens. At the same time, digital records of which sites patrons visit are squirreled away for eternity in official databases. Today, Chinese café patrons would be taking a big risk searching "Tibet and crackdown," and they know it.

The Panopticon Effect

But Web 2.0 technology posed a new problem for censors. By indexing data on remote servers rather than downloading it to the user's workstation, social networking sites like Facebook, Web-mail programs like Gmail and consumer sites like Netflix render themselves hard to watch. When almost all information online was transmitted by local Internet service providers and stored by local hosts, a government like Vietnam's could read data stored on a server in Ho Chi Minh City whenever it pleased—and respond by cutting off a user's access to that server. But Hanoi can't control what happens on Google servers in Mountain View, California. And it can't peek at every data packet going to and from America—the volume is too great.

Yet if governments can *convince* people that they are reading everything, they might not actually have to. And so the information-control agents from the world's most repressive regimes began thinking about what watchdogs call the "panopticon effect"—named for a type of prison conceived by the 18th-century social critic Jeremy Bentham. In it, a guard can watch the prisoners without their being able to tell whether he's watching. The question for authoritarians was the same: how do you make people feel as if they're being watched at all times and internalize the sense of omniscient [all-seeing] authority? A crude answer is the simple broadcast message. Xiao Qiang, the director of the China Internet Project, says that university functionaries might send a note to all students: "This weekend, public-security authorities will install security software on our system." He adds, "You don't know how well it works or what it does, but you certainly know every student is being warned." Or the authorities might send a text message like the one in Lhasa last week—a trick achieved by detecting which phones communicating with local Tibetan cell phone towers are roaming domestic subscribers.

Keep the Internet Unencumbered

Today, the Internet is both the vehicle and the battleground for freedom of expression around the world. The struggle between writers and governments over this free flow of information has escalated . . . and promises to intensify. Those supporting open frontiers for ideas and information need to be on high alert and take steps necessary to protect those silenced and to keep the Internet unencumbered.

Joanne Leedom-Ackerman,
"The Intensifying Battle over Internet Freedom,"
Christian Science Monitor, *February 24, 2009.*

Not Beyond the Law

Newer, automated methods are targeting individuals more directly. These methods are hard to track in detail because they are invariably deep official secrets, but experts believe China is the leading state practitioner right now. The most famous example is the avatar duo of Jingjing and Chacha (puns on the Chinese word for police), who appeared in early 2006. They are two adorable cartoon cops with big heads, big eyes and tight mouths in the anime [Japanese cartoon] style. They live on the home pages of several ISPs, or else they arrive, uninvited, on the screens of Chinese Netizens. If a Web surfer visits a domain that has elected to host the cartoon characters, Jingjing or Chacha may appear spontaneously to dispense amiable advice about online behavior. "We will send kind reminders to people to establish online safety and . . . to respect online laws and regulations by regulating themselves to create a healthy Internet circumstance and to maintain harmonious order," Jingjing says on his blog. Chen Minli, the head of Internet security and surveillance in the southern city of Shenzhen, explained the point of these Web cops to the Xinhua news service, driving home the panopticon effect: "The purpose is to let all Internet users know that the Internet is not a place beyond the law. The Internet police will maintain order in all online behaviors."

Other examples of ham-fisted surveillance—the kind meant to be noticed—have been chronicled by the OpenNet Initiative, a collaboration of several Western universities studying Internet freedoms. China is finding new and varied ways to apply its keyword-tracking technologies. First used to censor Web sites that contain certain phrases, they are now deployed to create the sensation that an intelligence agent is watching. The researchers report e-mails that sometimes arrive and sometimes don't, search engines that suddenly stop accepting particular queries, words that are sometimes excised and Web sites that arbitrarily become unavailable (browsers report a failure to connect or time out). For Netizens, it's impossible to know whether those effects represent censors typing away in a government data center or whether they're simply automated, like Jingjing and Chacha.

Strong-Arm Methods

The trick about the new repression isn't just getting people to think the government knows—or seems to know—what they're doing; it's making them believe they'll pay the price. Here the technology of Repression 2.0 melds with old-fashioned strong-arm methods: Those caught misbehaving are subjected to highly publicized character assassination, interrogation, threats to friends and families, trumped-up charges and show trials. Chinese police have shown up at the homes of Web surfers just minutes after they view an illicit site. Egyptian and Saudi courts try bloggers for sedition.

In the Middle East, censors are hunting not just for political challenges to the established order but also for signs of what they consider social deviancy, such as gay porn. But with so much ground to cover, resources are spread thin. So rather than convey a systematic sensation of surveillance, Middle Eastern governments are louder and angrier in their condemnations. Many Arab Internet service providers reluctantly share data about their clients' habits with authorities, fearing the consequences if they don't. Medhat Zayed owns a two-room Internet café in Cairo with six outdated PCs and one air conditioner. He and other proprietors are pressured to give daily reports on clients' browsing habits. "I don't want to spy," he says. "I don't want to play the role of the police . . . What I say can send them [to detention]. I hate what I'm doing, and it is *haram*"—proscribed by Muslim law. Yet he complies because of cases like Hala El-Masry, a 43-year-old woman from Egypt's conservative south who wrote a blog called Copts Without Borders, which chronicled cases of repression. Police detained her, accused her of plotting to kill her father and prosecuted her for undercutting national unity. Then authorities closed the two cafés from which she had posted blog items.

In the Middle East the overall effect is more erratic—it sometimes looks more like Repression 1.0—but no less terrifying than in China. "It's not a soft-power thing; it's imprisonment," says Ibrahim El-Houdaiby, an Egyptian blogger and dissident. In February, a popular Egyptian blogger who calls himself Kareem Amer got four years for insulting President Hosni Mubarak. And, El-Houdaiby warns, "they're still developing the technologies" used by China.

Examples of Repression

They are. Consider the case of Cairo blogger Wael Abbas, who is known in the Arab world for postings highly critical of Egyptian President Hosni Mubarak. He was well aware of how rough the regime could be on critics (he has posted videos of police torture sessions), but he was surprised one day to find his YouTube account closed—by YouTube. Droves of users had complained, in a short period, about the content he had uploaded. Who were they: The government? Ordinary Egyptians? Nobody really knew. YouTube eventually restored his account when Abbas convinced its operators he'd been targeted by the government. But then anonymous, false reports began circulating online that he had changed his religion three times (Protestant to Orthodox to Roman Catholic) and that he was gay. "You know how a conservative society like ours despises and hates whoever rotates between religions that easily, or an openly gay person," he says.

In China, by contrast, major ISPs are open about complying with directives from the Beijing Information Office to furnish data and ban keywords. In October, hours after Reporters Without Borders issued a report critical of Chinese Internet restrictions, the information office told ISPs to restrict keyword searches that included the group's name, the author's name and several phrases from the report; the ISPs obeyed within hours. Wang Jianzhou, the CEO of China's (and the world's) largest mobile-phone firm, China Mobile Communications Corp., is emblematic. When he was pressed at a news conference about the privacy implications of collecting user data, he said that "we never give this information away [to advertisers]. Only if the security authorities ask for it." . . .

The Next Step: Data Mining

The next step for governments struggling to keep up with the flow of dangerous data may be a technique called data mining. One possible model: the Total Information Awareness project, a post-9/11 U.S. Defense Department idea that, had it not been shut down by horrified lawmakers, would have analyzed patterns of writing, shopping, e-mailing and surfing among Web users. The notion wasn't to watch everything people said—it was to scan their online footprint for patterns that might point to criminals or terrorists. It's easy to imagine Beijing appropriating the concept when it can muster the computing power.

That would scare Web users for years. Technology has a way of constantly changing, but authoritarians of the world have at least one thing going for them: spreading fear is easy, and the Web makes it easier.

> *"There will be regimes who will try to shut down blogging, . . . but the evolution of the Internet has proved too rapid for governments to keep up with."*

Bloggers Evade Internet Censorship in Repressive Countries

Richard Seymour

Richard Seymour is a blogger and author who runs a Web site called Lenin's Tomb. In the following viewpoint, he argues that blogging is increasing in repressive countries, particularly in the Middle East, as an alternative way for citizens to communicate with one another and with the outside world. He contends that blogs are a form of subversive underground literature with the power to spark debate and unite people who share common political beliefs. In many cases, he insists, bloggers provide more accurate information about events in repressive countries than do mainstream journalists, who are subject to official censorship.

Richard Seymour, "Middle East Bloggers Set Cat Among the Pigeons," *Middle East*, vol. 388, April 2008, pp. 62–63. Copyright © 2008 IC Publications LTD. Reproduced by permission.

As you read, consider the following questions:

1. By what percentage has Internet usage in the Middle East grown since 2000, as reported by Richard Seymour?

2. Why do bloggers "keep it real," in the author's opinion?

3. What role did bloggers play during the 2007 Israeli-Lebanese conflict, according to Seymour?

The detention by Egyptian authorities of Internet blogger Abdel Kareem Nabil Soliman for publishing material critical of the Saudi regime—amongst other things—has once again brought the issue of the Internet and the Middle East to the forefront of debate. Soliman will serve four years behind bars for "contempt for religion, insulting the president and spreading false information".

Mr. Soliman's imprisonment followed the detention in Saudi Arabia of Fouad Al-Farhan. While the Saudi authorities have yet to reveal the charges against Al-Farhan, his supporters claim he fell foul of the police for publishing his often critical views of the regime on his blog, unusually, under his own name.

Blogs in the Middle East

A blog (a corruption of the term 'Web log') is a form of on-line diary where anyone with access to the Internet can create a platform from which they may reveal to the world whatever is on their minds. Often, these blogs contain little more than gentle musings, philosophical outpourings, poems and song lyrics, but they have proved to be a fertile ground for political thought and dissent. It is the potential for the latter that has alarmed some governments. About 2.5% of the world's Internet users come from the Middle East, where market penetration, with a 17.4% average, is a little lower than in many other areas of the world. Its growth since 2000 stands at 920% compared to an average 259% elsewhere.

Of the estimated 33.5m [million] Internet users in the Middle East only a small fraction publish blogs and, of these, political blogs contribute probably only a few thousand. Given that, it may seem that with such small numbers, the potential impact of the bloggers is limited. But has that not always been the way of political descent?

Subversive Underground Literature

In the 19th century, Karl Marx printed and distributed *The Communist Manifesto*, a subversive document if ever there was one, throughout Europe; and the Russian newspaper, *Pravda*, started life in the political underground, having to be smuggled into Russia and distributed secretly. Such newspapers and leaflets have galvanised political dissent across the world ever since and have often proved to have impacts that far outstrip their limited readership.

Political blogging has the potential to be the modern equivalent of subversive underground literature. While its direct reach may not go very far, it has the power to stimulate political debate, bringing together enough people to, if not shape—or even reflect—broader political opinions, at least create collective—and often inconvenient—interest where, before, there had been only lone voices in the wilderness. And all achievable for the price of an hour at an Internet café. No expensive printing press or distribution network is required. Clicking 'Submit' is all you need to do to make your views instantly available to the world.

While blogs have proved a useful tool for organising political movements, they have also often provided the outside world with a glimpse of life behind otherwise closed doors.

In the early days of the US-led invasion of Iraq, any sort of news about what was going on inside the country was difficult to come by. Western news organisations were spoon-fed information by military sources and censorship was considered a necessary evil. But where possible, bloggers got online to tell their inside stories, their personal tales of life before and after Saddam [Hussein, the former dictator of Iraq]. Some were hopeful, others were harrowing, but they each provided a valuable record of real Iraqi people as their country crumbled around them. It gave a voice to those who would otherwise have none.

Bloggers "Keep It Real"

It is true that bloggers are not bound by the traditional journalistic standards of truth and objectivity, but then, it seems, not all journalists feel that responsibility either. But in a medium that comes under no editorial control, and which grows dynamically around evolving events, patterns emerge. There is always the possibility of malicious individuals spreading false information but, as a whole, the general consensus of bloggers as a community is to "keep it real" in order not to be dismissed. Video footage and other evidence is frequently provided in order to substantiate the "voice" of the blogger.

Bloggers are less afraid to go where the mainstream media fear to tread. Shocking images of war that will never make it to television screens and newspapers in the West, have been distributed by bloggers and forwarded via e-mail all over the world.

Indeed, much political blogging is driven by, at best, a general disenchantment with the mainstream media and, at its most potent, outright hostility towards its reporting. This was never made more obvious than during the 2007 Israeli-Lebanese conflict when blogging as a news outlet really came into its own.

Despite the bombing, many Lebanese bloggers were able to continue posting and their reports were often at odds with what the mainstream media in the West were saying. And when the conflict zones became too dangerous to report from, then the mainstream media frequently reported on the bloggers' first-hand accounts, as if they were correspondents

World Internet Usage Statistics

World Regions	Internet Users Dec. 31, 2000	Internet Users March 31, 2009	Penetration (% population)	Users Growth 2000–2008	Users % of Table
Africa	4,514,400	54,171,500	5.6%	1,100.0%	3.4%
Asia	114,304,000	657,170,816	17.4%	474.9%	41.2%
Europe	105,096,093	393,373,398	48.9%	274.3%	24.6%
Middle East	3,284,800	45,861,346	23.3%	1,296.2%	2.9%
North America	108,096,800	251,290,489	74.4%	132.5%	15.7%
Latin America/Caribbean	18,068,919	173,619,140	29.9%	860.9%	10.9%
Oceania/Australia	7,620,480	20,783,419	60.4%	172.7%	1.3%
World Total	**360,985,492**	**1,596,270,108**	**23.8%**	**342.2%**	**100.0%**

TAKEN FROM: Internet World Stats, www.internetworldstats.com. Copyright © 2001–2009 Miniwatts Marketing Group.

in the field. The relationship between bloggers and the mainstream media is still uneasy, but both sides are recognising the potential of the other.

A Free Exchange of Ideas

But even the majority of blogs, which are not political in nature, are encouraging Internet users in the Middle East to express themselves freely—regardless of the topic being discussed—and exchange views with users all over the region and the world. Whether it be genteel discussion or ill-tempered clashes, ideas are being exchanged and alternative views considered, like never before.

So far in the Middle East, only young people with an interest in technology have switched on to blogs, though that is changing. Elsewhere in the world, politicians, journalists and commentators already make full use of blogging without, it has to be admitted, little cause for concern that what they write might land them in jail.

One social group that has benefited significantly from blogging is the region's women. With the mainstream media populated mostly by older men, young Middle Eastern women have turned to blogging to express their views publicly. While initial enthusiasm that this might lead to their emancipation has died away, the outlet for women, hitherto unheard from in some societies, remains.

Celebrity Bloggers

One famous blogger, going by the name of 'Riverbend' is an apparently well educated woman who kept up a running commentary of the situation within post-Saddam Baghdad until she left for the safety of Syria at which point the blogs stopped. In fact, the blogging phenomenon has seen a number of celebrities created among the well-known bloggers who attract a large following. One such celebrity is known as Salam Pax, whose blogs from Baghdad led to him being tracked down and recruited by a British newspaper for whom he briefly worked.

There will be regimes who will try to shut down blogging, and to some extent they will succeed; but the evolution of the Internet has proved too rapid for governments to keep up with and the drivers of that development often find themselves a step ahead of the authorities. With technology there is always a way. And no regime has ever succeeded in silencing everybody.

> *"Being inside China means operating under the sweeping rules that govern all forms of media here: guidance from the authorities; the threat of financial ruin or time in jail; the unavoidable self-censorship."*

China's Internet Censorship Is Effective

James Fallows

China is frequently cited as one of the most censorious countries in the world. The government's system for blocking citizens' access to Web sites it deems subversive or contrary to its official message is known as the "Great Firewall of China." In the following viewpoint, James Fallows, a national correspondent for the Atlantic *magazine, contends that China's Great Firewall can be breached fairly easily. He maintains, however, that the system makes defying the censors just difficult enough to dissuade most citizens from doing it. As a result, Fallows concludes, free speech in China will remain squelched for the foreseeable future.*

James Fallows, "The Connection Has Been Reset," *Atlantic*, March 2008, pp. 64–70. Copyright © 2009 The Atlantic Media Co., as first published in the Atlantic Magazine. Distributed by Tribune Media Services. Reproduced by permission.

As you read, consider the following questions:

1. How do Chinese authorities monitor Internet traffic, as reported by James Fallows?

2. Why do authorities refrain from shutting down proxies and virtual private networks (VPNs), according to the author?

3. Why do Chinese bloggers prefer to operate within the Chinese firewall, according to Fallows?

Depending on how you look at it, the Chinese government's attempt to rein in the Internet is crude and slapdash or ingenious and well-crafted. When American technologists write about the control system, they tend to emphasize its limits. When Chinese citizens discuss it—at least with me—they tend to emphasize its strength. All of them are right, which makes the government's approach to the Internet a nice proxy for its larger attempt to control people's daily lives.

Disappointingly, "Great Firewall" [a term commonly used to describe China's Internet censorship system] is not really the right term for the Chinese government's overall control strategy. China has indeed erected a firewall—a barrier to keep its Internet users from dealing easily with the outside world—but that is only one part of a larger, complex structure of monitoring and censorship. The official name for the entire approach, which is ostensibly a way to keep hackers and other rogue elements from harming Chinese Internet users, is the "Golden Shield Project." Since that term is too creepy to bear repeating, I'll use "the control system" for the overall strategy, which includes the "Great Firewall of China," or GFW, as the means of screening contact with other countries.

Choke Points and Mirrors

In America, the Internet was originally designed to be free of choke points, so that each packet of information could be routed quickly around any temporary obstruction. In China, the Internet came with choke points built in. Even now, virtually all Internet contact between China and the rest of the world is routed through a very small number of fiber-optic cables that enter the country at one of three points: the Beijing-Qingdao-Tianjin area in the north, where cables come in from Japan; Shanghai on the central coast, where they also come from Japan; and Guangzhou in the south, where they come from Hong Kong. (A few places in China have Internet service via satellite, but that is both expensive and slow. Other lines run across central Asia to Russia but carry little traffic.) In late 2006, Internet users in China were reminded just how important these choke points are when a seabed earthquake near Taiwan cut some major cables serving the country. It took months before international transmissions to and from most of China regained even their pre-quake speed, such as it was.

Thus Chinese authorities can easily do something that would be harder in most developed countries: physically monitor all traffic into or out of the country. They do so by installing at each of these few "international gateways" a device called a "tapper" or "network sniffer," which can mirror every packet of data going in or out. This involves mirroring in both a figurative and a literal sense. "Mirroring" is the term for normal copying or backup operations, and in this case real though extremely small mirrors are employed. Information travels along fiber-optic cables as little pulses of light, and as these travel through the Chinese gateway routers, numerous tiny mirrors bounce reflections of them to a separate set of "Golden Shield" computers. Here the term's creepiness is appropriate. As the other routers and servers (short for file servers, which are essentially very large-capacity computers) that make up the Internet do their best to get the packet where it's supposed to go, China's own surveillance computers are looking over the same information to see whether it should be stopped. . . .

Getting Around the Wall

As a practical matter, anyone in China who wants to get around the firewall can choose between two well-known and dependable alternatives: the proxy server and the VPN. A proxy server is a way of connecting your computer inside China with another one somewhere else—or usually to a series of foreign computers, automatically passing signals along to conceal where they really came from. You initiate a Web request, and the proxy system takes over, sending it to a computer in America or Finland or Brazil. Eventually the system finds what you want and sends it back. The main drawback is that it makes Internet operations very, very slow. But because most proxies cost nothing to install and operate, this is the favorite of students and hackers in China.

A VPN, or virtual private network, is a faster, fancier, and more elegant way to achieve the same result. Essentially a VPN creates your own private, encrypted channel that runs alongside the normal Internet. From within China, a VPN connects you with an Internet server somewhere else. You pass your browsing and downloading requests to that American or Finnish or Japanese server, and it finds and sends back what you're looking for. The GFW doesn't stop you, because it can't read the encrypted messages you're sending. Every foreign business operating in China uses such a network. VPNs are freely advertised in China, so individuals can sign up, too. I use one that costs $40 per year. (An expat in China thinks: *that's a little over a dime a day*. A Chinese factory worker thinks: *it's a week's take-home pay*. Even for a young academic, it's a couple days' work.)

As a technical matter, China could crack down on the proxies and VPNs whenever it pleased. Today the policy is: if a message comes through that the surveillance system cannot read because it's encrypted, let's wave it on through! Obviously the system's behavior could be reversed. But everyone I spoke with said that China could simply not afford to crack down that way. "Every bank, every foreign manufacturing company, every retailer, every software vendor needs VPNs to exist," a Chinese professor told me. "They would have to shut down the next day if asked to send their commercial information through the regular Chinese Internet and the Great Firewall." Closing down the free, easy-to-use proxy servers would create a milder version of the same problem. Encrypted e-mail, too, passes through the GFW without scrutiny, and users of many Web-based mail systems can establish a secure session simply by typing "https:" rather than the usual "http:" in a site's address—for instance, https://mail.yahoo.com. To keep China in business, then, the government has to allow some exceptions to its control efforts—even knowing that many Chinese citizens will exploit the resulting loopholes.

A Doomed Effort?

Because the Chinese government can't plug every gap in the Great Firewall, many American observers have concluded that its larger efforts to control electronic discussion, and the democratization and grassroots organizing it might nurture, are ultimately doomed. A recent item on an influential American tech Web site had the headline "Chinese National Firewall Isn't All That Effective." In October [2007], *Wired* ran a story under the headline "The Great Firewall: China's Misguided—and Futile—Attempt to Control What Happens Online."

Let's not stop to discuss why the vision of democracy-through-communications-technology is so convincing to so many Americans. (Samizdat [handwritten copies of censored publications], fax machines, and the Voice of America eventually helped bring down the Soviet system. Therefore proxy servers and online chat rooms must erode the power of the Chinese state. Right?) Instead, let me emphasize how unconvincing this vision is to most people who deal with China's system of extensive, if imperfect, Internet controls.

China's "Mental Firewall"

China's 162 million Internet users are a largely young and wealthy set who typically aren't engaged in politics. . . .

But when content does get political, the government doesn't have to do all the censoring itself. Behind the Great Firewall, it relies on Internet companies to take down content that might offend the party or risk their business licenses.

A third line is self-censorship. Isaac Mao, a blogging pioneer in China, has dubbed this problem China's "mental firewall."

Geoffrey A. Fowler,
"Bloggers in China Start Testing Limits of 'Mental Firewall,'"
Wall Street Journal, *December 5, 2007.*

Think again of the real importance of the Great Firewall. Does the Chinese government really care if a citizen can look up the Tiananmen Square entry on Wikipedia? Of course not. Anyone who wants that information will get it—by using a proxy server or VPN, by e-mailing to a friend overseas, even by looking at the surprisingly broad array of foreign magazines that arrive, uncensored, in Chinese public libraries.

Keeping People Inside

What the government cares about is making the quest for information just enough of a nuisance that people generally won't bother. Most Chinese people, like most Americans, are interested mainly in their own country. All around them is more information about China and things Chinese than they could possibly take in. The newsstands are bulging with papers and countless glossy magazines. The bookstores are big, well stocked, and full of patrons, and so are the public libraries. Video stores, with pirated versions of anything. Lots of TV channels. And of course the Internet, where sites in Chinese and about China constantly proliferate. When this much is available inside the Great Firewall, why go to the expense and bother, or incur the possible risk, of trying to look outside?

All the technology employed by the Golden Shield, all the marvelous mirrors that help build the Great Firewall—these and other modern achievements matter mainly for an old-fashioned and pre-technological reason. By making the search for external information a nuisance, they drive Chinese people back to an environment in which familiar tools of social control come into play.

Chinese bloggers have learned that if they want to be read in China, they must operate within China, on the same side of the firewall as their potential audience. Sure, they could put up exactly the same information outside the Chinese mainland. But according to Rebecca MacKinnon, a former Beijing correspondent for CNN now at the Journalism and Media Studies Center of the University of Hong Kong, their readers won't make the effort to cross the GFW and find them. "If you want to have traction in China, you have to *be* in China," she told me. And being inside China means operating under the sweeping rules that govern all forms of media here: guidance from the authorities; the threat of financial ruin or time in jail; the unavoidable self-censorship as the cost of defiance sinks in.

Most blogs in China are hosted by big Internet companies. Those companies know that the government will hold them responsible if a blogger says something bad. Thus the companies, for their own survival, are dragooned [forced] into service as auxiliary censors.

The Censor Squad

Large teams of paid government censors delete offensive comments and warn errant bloggers. (No official figures are available, but the censor workforce is widely assumed to number in the tens of thousands.) Members of the public at large are encouraged to speak up when they see subversive material. The propaganda ministries send out frequent instructions about what can and cannot be discussed. In October [2007], the group Reporters Without Borders, based in Paris, released an astonishing report by a Chinese Internet technician writing under the pseudonym "Mr. Tao." He collected dozens of the messages he and other Internet operators had received from the central government. Here is just one, from the summer of 2006:

> 17 June 2006, 18:35
>
> From: Chen Hua, deputy director of the Beijing Internet Information Administrative Bureau
>
> Dear colleagues, the Internet has of late been full of articles and messages about the death of a Shenzhen engineer, Hu Xinyu, as a result of overwork. All sites must stop posting articles on this subject, those that have already been posted about it must be removed from the site and, finally, forums and blogs must withdraw all articles and messages about this case.

"Domestic censorship is the real issue, and it is about social control, human surveillance, peer pressure, and self-censorship," Xiao Qiang of Berkeley says. Last fall, a team of computer scientists from the University of California at Davis and the University of New Mexico published an exhaustive technical analysis of the GFW's operation and of the ways it could be foiled. But they stressed a nontechnical factor: "The presence of censorship, even if easy to evade, promotes self-censorship."

Forbidden Topics Persist

It would be wrong to portray China as a tightly buttoned mind-control state. It is too wide-open in too many ways for that. "Most people in China feel freer than any Chinese people have been in the country's history, ever," a Chinese software engineer who earned a doctorate in the United States told me. "There has never been a space for any kind of discussion before, and the government is clever about continuing to expand space for anything that doesn't threaten its survival." But it would also be wrong to ignore the cumulative effect of topics people are not allowed to discuss. "Whether or not Americans supported George W. Bush, they could not *avoid* learning about Abu Ghraib," Rebecca MacKinnon says. In China, "the controls mean that whole topics inconvenient for the regime simply don't exist in public discussion." Most Chinese people remain wholly unaware of internationally noticed issues like, for instance, the controversy over the Three Gorges Dam [a hydroelectric dam on the Yangtze River that forced the relocation of more than 1 million people and has been criticized for harming the environment].

Countless questions about today's China boil down to: How long can this go on? How long can the industrial growth continue before the natural environment is destroyed? How long can the super-rich get richer, without the poor getting mad? And so on through a familiar list. The Great Firewall poses the question in another form: How long can the regime control what people are allowed to know, without the people caring enough to object? On current evidence, for quite a while.

| "*Many bloggers feel that Western, particularly American, concerns about censorship in China are blown out of proportion.*"

China's Internet Censorship Can Be Circumvented

April Gu

In the following viewpoint, April Gu argues that many Internet users are successfully evading censorship in China. She acknowledges that the Chinese government's censorship system is formidable and that Chinese citizens routinely self-censor. She insists, however, that many users—particularly young bloggers—are increasingly engaged in free exchanges of information, some of which have pressured the government to moderate its repressive policies and actions. Gu, a graduate of New York University's Stern School of Business, wrote this viewpoint while doing research in Beijing on a Fulbright Fellowship.

As you read, consider the following questions:

1. How many bloggers are there in China compared to the United States, as reported by April Gu?

April Gu, "In China, Bloggers Often Circumvent Censorship," *Star-Ledger* (Newark, NJ), May 13, 2007, p. 1. Copyright © 2007 The Star-Ledger. All rights reserved. Reproduced by permission.

2. How does the story of Gao Yaojie illustrate the power of blogs, in the author's opinion?

3. Why did one television anchorman/blogger call for the closure of Starbucks in the Forbidden City, according to Gu?

For information as sensitive as local government corruption or the spread of a disease, most Chinese turn to blogs, not newspapers.

Five years ago, blogs were still largely unheard of in China. Today, China is home to over 20 million bloggers. By contrast, the United States lags behind at 12 million bloggers.

Chinese Bloggers

In January [2007], journalist Wang Keqin investigated the murder of a reporter, Lan Chengzhang, who was beaten to death when he allegedly threatened to uncover an illegal coal mine. But his story was heavily censored before it was printed. Undaunted, Wang posted the full version on his blog.

A few weeks later, Gao Yaojie, an 80-year-old doctor who uncovered the atrocious blood bank practices that led to the mass spread of AIDS in Henan province, wrote about her house arrest on her blog.

She was being prevented by authorities from traveling to the United States to receive an award for her activism. Within hours, her entry was pulled down but the news had already broken. As international pressure grew intense, the Chinese government allowed Gao to visit Washington, D.C., in March [2007].

After her return, she posted a photograph on her blog of her meeting with Sen. Hillary Clinton [now secretary of state]. Gao also regularly posts items about the AIDS crisis and offers her thoughts on sex-education strategies around the world.

Virtual Room to Breathe

Chinese bloggers tend to be highly educated urbanites living in technologically savvy cities like Beijing, Shanghai or Guangzhou. Unlike Gao, however, bloggers, like Internet users in general, are usually young; more than half are between 18 and 30.

Asked why blogs are so popular, Hu Bei Bei, a graduate student at the Chinese Academy of Social Sciences in Beijing, said, "I started blogging because I really enjoy the feeling that one space could completely be counted as mine."

Living in some of the most densely populated cities in the world, young Chinese turn to blogs for room to breathe and relax, even if that room is only virtual.

But as blogs allow news to be transmitted much more easily and quickly, this generation is increasingly turning away from traditional media such as newspapers or television that are more susceptible to propaganda and government control.

In a January 2007 survey by the China Internet Network Information Center, 85 percent of responders said they used the Internet as a "main approach" to receive information. More than one-fourth reported they frequently read or wrote blogs.

"The spread of blogs is of course a good thing," said Chen Bi Bo, a student at Tsinghua, one of the premiere universities in China. He writes a blog about the economy.

"In China, any channel that allows the masses to speak up should be encouraged. Any opinions should be discussed openly; this will enable news to be more transparent, cut down on incomplete reporting, and even decrease production costs of educational materials. Of course, at the same time this will bolster our ability to supervise the government."

Official Censorship

However, in a country with a policy of rigorous political censorship, it is usually the other way around. Numerous bloggers have run into trouble as a result of their content.

Hungry for Information

In 2002 ... I started a private company in the United States that relies on a network of hundreds of volunteers, inside China and abroad, to produce technologies to defeat Internet censorship. ...

Our volunteers have proved again and again that we can defeat even China's costly technologies and its legions of Internet police. Chinese citizens are hungry for uncensored information. When we first launched, one excited user sent us a message that read, simply, "Thank you"—repeated hundreds of times.

Bill Xia,
"Foiling Beijing's Cyber Cops,"
Los Angeles Times, *July 3, 2006.*

Early last year a highly publicized case involved the shutdown of an MSN Spaces blog after the company's affiliate in Shanghai received complaints about its entries from authorities. The blog's writer had discussed sensitive issues, including the firing of an unusually blunt editor at a Beijing newspaper.

MSN Spaces has also intermittently blocked users from using words such as "democracy" and "freedom" in their blog titles.

It is estimated that China employs 30,000 people to troll through Web sites, discussion boards and chat rooms looking for suspect material. Sites such as BBC News, Wikipedia and Blogspot, a popular U.S.-based domain for bloggers, as well as various others, are regularly banned. Posts are closely monitored and will be deleted if considered anti-government. Additionally, users are required to register their real identities if they set up blogs using their own server space.

A Challenge to Government

But blogs still remain troublesome for authorities who wish to restrict free speech. The Press and Publication Administration announced last month [April 2007] that, due to the proliferation of blogs and Web casts, new regulations will soon be drawn up to ensure "a more healthy and active Internet environment."

Although privacy infringement was cited as a main concern, the potential influence of blogging has led the government to be wary of its power.

Recently a blog written by a television anchorman generated enormous support for the closure of a Starbucks outlet in the Forbidden City after he asserted that it "tramples over Chinese culture." Half a million followers signed his online petition calling for the Starbucks to be removed. A decision will be made about the outlet's fate in June. [The store was closed in July 2007.]

Self-Censorship Continues

Don't hold your breath for an explosion of democracy and free speech, however. While the power of blogs is undeniable, they won't be able to make much of an impact unless more bloggers feel free to write what they want. Knowing what topics are best avoided, most Chinese don't even bother to touch on them.

"My blog is purely about academic matters and there is not a strong tendency toward politics, so I haven't experienced censorship. But I feel that the very existence of censorship leads to a restricted zone even within academic research. This results in self-selection because no academics will research restricted topics; because there is no research of these topics, they aren't technically censored," said Chen.

The vast majority of blogs serve as makeshift diaries, hold few contentious opinions and have no impact on the news.

The most widely read blogs, as tracked by Zhuaxia, an online service that tracks RSS [really simple syndication] feeds [a format for publishing frequently updated news], are mainly about information technology and the dramas of private, everyday life. There were no blogs dedicated solely to political or economic news among the top 10.

Still, many bloggers feel that Western, particularly American, concerns about censorship in China are blown out of proportion. Zhang Peng has written two blogs, one about her daily experiences and the other on technology. She acknowledged that censorship restricts some rights, but added, "In a developing country with a population of 1.3 billion, this is at present one of the best methods of uniting the people's ideology. So my advice to America is, take care of yourself."

> *"Some of the world's most famous Internet companies have lined up to show China how to cripple the Web."*

U.S. Companies Are Abetting Internet Censorship in China

Jonathan Mirsky

In the following viewpoint, Jonathan Mirsky argues that many Western technology companies—including the U.S. companies Google, Microsoft, and Yahoo!—are helping the Chinese government to censor its citizens. By selling routers and filtering programs to the Chinese government, Mirsky contends, these companies are complicit in the tyrannical suppression of speech and other democratic freedoms in China. Mirsky is a journalist and historian specializing in Chinese affairs.

As you read, consider the following questions:

1. What topics are Chinese citizens forbidden to research on the Internet, according to Jonathan Mirsky?

2. How does the case of Shi Tao illustrate the harmful role of Western Internet companies in China, as described by the author?

Jonathan Mirsky, "China's Tyranny Has the Best Hi-Tech Help," *International Herald-Tribune*, January 16, 2006, p. 6. Copyright © 2006 by International Herald Tribune. Reprinted with permission.

3. Why should Americans care about the role Western technology companies are playing in China, according to Rebecca MacKinnon, as quoted by Mirsky?

You can find anything you want on China's Internet: sex, fashion, business, travel, entertainment, romance. Anything, that is, except democracy, Tiananmen, Taiwan, human rights, Tibet and hundreds of other subjects.

Chinese searching the Internet for key, or "black" words are likely to be arrested, tried and imprisoned for up to 10 years on charges of subversion, revealing state secrets or spreading propaganda injurious to the state. They meet a similar fate if they use "black" words in something they post on the Internet, especially for foreigners to read.

State Censorship

This is the biggest campaign of state censorship that has ever been carried out, John Palfrey, executive director of the Berkman Center for Internet and Society at Harvard Law School, testified to Congress last April [2005]. Fear, he said, "has led the Chinese government to create the world's most sophisticated Internet filtering regime."

This surveillance and blocking, Harvard experts have found, extends over tens of thousands of sites. "China's system prevents users from accessing most politically sensitive content on the Internet," Palfrey said in his testimony, "including information about opposition political groups, independence movements, the Falun Gong spiritual movement, the Dalai Lama [the spiritual leader of Tibet] and the Tiananmen Square incident [1989 massacre of pro-democracy demonstrators]."

Some Westerners will shrug their shoulders, filing Internet censorship in their mental index of Chinese human rights violations. Despite its rapid economic expansion, they presume, China is at best a second world country when it comes to sophisticated technology.

Helping the Censors

But Beijing has the very best help. Some of the world's most famous Internet companies have lined up to show China how to cripple the Web.

A partial list includes Google, Microsoft, Yahoo!, Cisco, Sun Microsystems and Skype. Each has its expertise. Google removes from its Chinese site whatever the Chinese deem politically sensitive. According to Reporters without Frontiers [an organization that promotes free press worldwide], "Cisco Systems has sold several thousand routers to enable the regime to build an online spying system and the firm's engineers have helped set it to spot 'subversive' key words in messages."

In 2002, Yahoo! signed a document called a "Public Pledge on Self-Discipline for the Chinese Internet Industry." That agreement led to disaster for Shi Tao. Shi, 37, worked for a business daily. On April 30, last year [2005], he was sentenced to 10 years behind bars for revealing a top state secret, to foreign Web sites. The secret was an official warning to the news media on the threat to China posed by dissidents returning to mark the 15th anniversary of the Tiananmen killings. Yahoo! and Cisco furnished the technology that permitted the security services to identify Shi.

According to Joseph Kahn in the *New York Times*, "Shi's case alarmed critics of the Chinese government because his posting did not reveal the sender or the source of the information. . . . Using investigative techniques that were not revealed during Shi's trial, Beijing state security officials pinpointed the Chinese source of the e-mail."

Corporate Justifications

All the American companies helping the Chinese police state insist they are merely obeying local laws. A Cisco spokesman said, "Our perspective is that it's the user, not Cisco, that determines the functionality and uses to which the technology is put."

Google's spokesman stated that defying could result in Google News being kept out of China altogether and losing millions of dollars worth of business. "The trade-off," he explained, is in the "best interests of our users located in China."

Yahoo's chief executive officer also justified his company's actions: "It's just really important for us to have good relations and good partnerships with governments all over the world."

"This is a complex and difficult issue," said Brooke Richardson, of Microsoft. "We think it's better to be there with our services than not be there."

Optimists in the West suggest that Chinese economic reform will soon be followed by political reform. There is little evidence for this. President Hu Jintao is more repressive than his predecessor. Most of the Chinese returning from Harvard, Oxford and the Sorbonne will dissolve into the vast sea of Chinese whose view of the world is shaped by the Communist Party.

The Impact for Americans

But should we care what Chinese are reading on the Internet? John Palfrey of Harvard is blunt: "The ramifications of this censorship regime should be of concern to anyone who believes in participatory democracy. How the Chinese government restricts its citizens' online interactions is significantly altering the global Internet landscape."

Americans who think that in any event China is far away may be jolted by this suggestion from Rebecca MacKinnon, a former foreign correspondent in China now specializing in Internet censorship: "If these American technology companies have so few moral qualms about giving in to Chinese government demands to hand over Chinese user data or censor Chinese people's content, can we be sure they won't do the same thing in response to potentially illegal demands by an overzealous government agency in our own country? Or will we all sit there like frogs in water being brought very slowly to a boil?"

"The presence of U.S. technology titans in China makes it more likely, not less, that people will be free to exercise their rights."

U.S. Companies Are Promoting Internet Freedom in China

Clyde Wayne Crews Jr. and Peter Suderman

In the following viewpoint, Clyde Wayne Crews Jr. and Peter Suderman reject the argument that American technology companies such as Google, Cisco, and Yahoo! are helping the Chinese government censor its citizens. In fact, the authors insist, by providing superior Western technology to China, U.S. firms are improving the prospects for expanded democratic freedoms in the Communist country. Crews is vice president of policy and director of technology studies at the Competitive Enterprise Institute (CEI), a libertarian think tank. Suderman is former assistant editorial director at CEI and writes on technology, media, and culture for various publications.

Clyde Wayne Crews Jr. and Peter Suderman, "U.S. Tech: Get to China," *Washington Times*, March 1, 2006, p. A19. Copyright © Washington Time Library Mar 1, 2006. Reproduced by permission.

As you read, consider the following questions:

1. How many people in China have Internet access, according to the authors?

2. What are the benefits of Google's presence in China, as stated by Clyde Wayne Crews Jr. and Peter Suderman?

3. In what ways will Western companies create pressure for change in China, according to the authors?

We once scorned the idea the Internet could be censored. Many politicians have tried to stop porn, but always to no avail. Spam still pours in our in-boxes, and the Net is increasingly susceptible to viruses and "malware."

Despite the tough-talkin' rhetoric and angry hand-wringing of authorities, there are very few actual limits to what people can do online. Even in its more restricted forms, the Net fosters an array of features that enable free expression.

This means the recent attack by human rights activists and some legislators on U.S. technology firms like Google, Microsoft and Yahoo! isn't just misguided—it's a direct threat to the spread of freedom. Ban-happy Chinese censors, not U.S. companies, should be the target of the activists' ire.

These firms—under fire for "censoring" search results and blocking some Web logs at the behest of Chinese censors—provide services that foster anonymous communications.

Leaving China disconnected, as some suggest, would hinder developing Internet infrastructure and would deny Chinese citizens access to the many useful services these companies provide. Just 110 million people out of China's 1.4 billion now have Net access; there's still a monumental "digital divide." Most Chinese citizens do not experience a limited or censored Internet, but no Internet at all.

For those who have Web access, there often are ways around government restrictions. "Hacktivists" worldwide already provide escape hatches from Chinese government censorship.

Chipping Away at State Power

China is not the police state that its leaders sometimes would like it to be; the Communist Party's monopoly on information is crumbling, and its monopoly on power will follow. The Internet is chipping away relentlessly at the Party. . . . With the Internet, China is developing for the first time in 4,000 years of history a powerful independent institution that offers checks and balances on the emperors.

Nicholas D. Kristof,
*"In China It's ****** vs. Netizens,"*
New York Times, *June 20, 2006.*

The Web, given its architecture, is famous for routing around censorship as if it were a physical disruption. Morally and technologically, staying put and fighting for change—not pulling out—is the right course of action.

Compulsory blocking of Web sites does not outweigh the profound good tech firms can otherwise do in China. Google, for example, heralds vastly more than its search capability. Google's ejection would hurt the cause of human rights: free Google talk, free Gmail accounts (which can facilitate anonymous communications through password sharing), and the free gigabyte of storage that comes with Gmail accounts (which would have cost huge sums not long ago) all have profound "subversive" implications that can vastly outweigh the negatives from restricted searches. Even if some sites are blocked, the total network access for the Chinese is increased.

Blame must lie with Chinese censors. Tech firms want to promote information, and have no inherent interest in censoring information they profit by providing. The presence of U.S.

technology titans in China makes it more likely, not less, that people will be free to exercise their rights.

Economic freedom—here, the fostering of peer networking and individual broadcasting—facilitates political freedom.

Even in the West, the graphical Web is relatively new. It would be foolish to fight so hard to achieve the current unprecedented levels of free speech in China only to pull back because success is not yet complete. The answer is not to deprive Chinese citizens of what Google and others can provide.

Companies need to be relentless rather than apologetic, because the tides of morality, technology and history are on their side. More international companies in China will create more pressure for change—not just from these external forces, but also from the profound employment opportunities (and derivative entrepreneurship) that would accrue to China if "big tech" makes a big footprint.

The fact China allows Internet access at all is the camel's nose under the tent. The aim now should be to push for more openness, enlisting other tech companies, activists, and governments to urge changes in China's policies.

Companies can't fight it alone. They need to team up to refuse, and the U.S. government can get involved in what is essentially a foreign-policy and law-enforcement matter. The State Department already has a Global Internet Freedom Task Force.

Google's oft-derided slogan is "Don't Be Evil"; in this case, it's living up to that credo. Google, Microsoft and other firms are not violating rights—instead they are doing more than nearly anyone else to assure the Chinese of tomorrow enjoy full individual rights. Technology firms are not to blame for the failings of a foreign government; the moral outrage belongs with Chinese censors.

Periodical Bibliography

The following articles have been selected to supplement the diverse views presented in this chapter.

Roby Alampay "You Block YouTube at Your Peril," *International Herald Tribune*, April 12, 2007.

Patrick J. Buchanan "Return of the Censors," *Human Events*, June 17, 2008. www.humanevents.com.

Peter Burrows "Internet Censorship: A Community Effort," *Business Week*, November 20, 2008.

Christian Science Monitor "Open China's Great Firewall," July 24, 2008.

Gady A. Epstein "Dark Journalism," *Forbes*, July 21, 2008.

Alastair Gee "Russia's Dissident Bloggers Fear for Their Lives," *U.S. News & World Report Online*, September 30, 2008. www.usnews.com.

Sally Jenkins "Speak Up, and Get Shut Down," *Washington Post*, August 6, 2008.

Garry Kasparov "How Putin Muzzled Russia's Press," *Wall Street Journal*, June 27, 2008.

Nicholas D. Kristof "Slipping over the Great Firewall of China," *New York Times*, August 24, 2008.

Joanne Leedom-Ackerman "The Intensifying Battle over Internet Freedom," *Christian Science Monitor*, February 24, 2009.

Don Podesta "The Rise of Soft Censorship," *Washington Post*, February 2, 2009.

Peter Savodnik "Postcard: Moscow," *TIME*, March 13, 2008.

Bill Xia "Foiling Beijing's Cyber Cops," *Los Angeles Times*, July 3, 2006.

OPPOSING VIEWPOINTS® SERIES

CHAPTER 4

Is Freedom in the United States Threatened by Censorship?

Chapter Preface

Most Americans take their freedom of speech for granted, enjoying the right to read, write, and say almost whatever they want without fear of government reprisals. Even in the United States, however, with its First Amendment protections, freedom of speech is not absolute. It is a crime to shout "Fire!" in a crowded theater in the absence of a fire, or to use speech to intentionally provoke violence, or to advocate the violent overthrow of the government. Moreover, children and teenagers do not possess the same free speech rights as adults. The U.S. Supreme Court has determined, for example, that high school journalists do not have the same rights as professional, adult journalists.

Prior to 1988, student journalists enjoyed First Amendment protection essentially on par with adults. Their free speech rights had been established in the 1969 Supreme Court decision *Tinker v. Des Moines Independent Community School District*. The *Tinker* case involved three students from Des Moines, Idaho, who in 1965 wore black armbands to school to protest the Vietnam War. When the school administrators asked them to remove the armbands, the students refused. They were suspended, and their case eventually reached the Supreme Court. The Court ruled seven to two that forcing the students to remove the armbands violated their First Amendment right to free speech. This decision was based on the premise that wearing the armbands was a form of symbolic speech. Although speech can be restricted in the school environment, the Court acknowledged that wearing the armbands was not a significant enough disruption to justify such a limitation on the students' rights. As the Court famously put it, students and teachers do not "shed their constitutional rights to freedom of speech or expression at the schoolhouse gate."

The *Tinker* decision set a precedent for a relatively permissive view of students' free speech rights until 1988, when the Supreme Court decided *Hazelwood School District et al. v. Kuhlmeier et al.* This case stemmed from the decision of a high school principal to remove two stories—one on divorce and one on teen pregnancy—from a school newspaper because he believed that they were inappropriate for younger students. In a five-to-three decision, the Court sided with the principal, holding that the First Amendment rights confirmed in *Tinker* did not require a public school to endorse speech that is contrary to its "legitimate pedagogical goals." In addition, the Court ruled that a school publication that is not a "public forum"—designed by policy and practice to provide a platform for students' opinions—is entitled to a lower level of First Amendment protection than one that is a public forum.

In response to the *Hazelwood* decision, more than ten states have passed laws (sometimes called "anti-*Hazelwood* laws") that protect the First Amendment rights of high school journalists. In addition, a 2004 federal district court case, *Dean v. Utica Community Schools*, afforded expanded First Amendment protection to high school journalists, but only in one district of the state of Michigan. The case involved a story written by student Katy Dean about a husband and wife who were suing the Utica School District, alleging that fumes from the district's idling school busses had caused the husband's lung cancer and other illnesses. The school's principal killed the story on the grounds that it was of poor quality. District Court Judge Arthur J. Tarnow, however, ruled that this act of censorship was "indefensible." He concluded that the school paper in this case was a limited public forum and therefore worthy of First Amendment protection. Furthermore, contrary to the principal's claim, Judge Tarnow concluded that the article was well written and was only censored because the principal disagreed with its content. Because the *Dean* case was heard in a district court rather than the Supreme Court, it did not overturn *Hazelwood*. It did set a precedent, however, that might influence other cases in the future.

High school journalism is just one topic of debate when it comes to freedom of speech in America. Other contentious issues considered in this chapter include book banning, flag desecration, and the regulation of talk radio.

> "*Everyone knows some librarians bypass good books. . . . The reasons range from a book's sexual content and gay themes to its language and violence.*"

Books Are Being Banned in the United States

Debra Lau Whelan

Debra Lau Whelan is a senior editor for School Library Journal, *a publication that features book reviews and articles on developments in the school library profession. In the following viewpoint, she argues that books are routinely censored in public and school libraries. Not only are books removed in response to challenges by parents and other citizens, Lau Whelan maintains, they are also excluded by librarians who fear that their presence might incite protest. The author concludes that librarians should uphold their professional ideals of intellectual freedom and oppose this form of self-censorship.*

As you read, consider the following questions:

1. How many written challenges to books were there in 2007, as reported by the author?

Debra Lau Whelan, "A Dirty Little Secret: Self-Censorship," School Library Journal, February 1, 2009. Copyright © 2009. Reproduced from School Library Journal. A Cahners/ R.R. Bowker Publication, by permission.

2. What percentage of librarians have dealt with a book challenge, according to the research cited by Debra Lau Whelan?

3. According to the Arkansas study referred to by the author, what percentage of libraries in that state have books with gay story lines?

When Barry Lyga finished writing his second young adult (YA) novel, he knew there'd be trouble. After all, *Boy Toy* was about a 12-year-old who has sex with a beautiful teacher twice his age, and Lyga expected it to spark letters to local papers, trigger complaints to the school board, and incite some parents to yank it off library shelves.

But none of those things ever happened.

"The book just didn't get out there," says Lyga. "Kids weren't getting the book because adults weren't letting them get the book."

At first, that didn't make much sense. *Boy Toy* (2007) was getting rave reviews from professional journals, and the *New York Times*, the *Los Angeles Times*, and *USA Today* loved it. So did the kid-lit bloggers who gave *Boy Toy* the Cybil Award for best YA fiction. Yet its sales figures were lower than Lyga's first novel, *The Astonishing Adventures of Fanboy and Goth Girl*.

Then the news started trickling in.

Some bookstores were placing the novel in the adult section, while others weren't carrying it at all. Soon Lyga started hearing stories about librarians who loved the book but refused to recommend or buy it, just in case someone complained. There was even an e-mail from a high school media specialist in Maryland who was so nuts about *Boy Toy* that she read it three times—but ultimately decided not to include it in her collection.

Soft Censorship

"It's sort of a soft, quiet, very insidious censorship, where nobody is raising a stink, nobody is complaining, nobody is burning books," says Lyga about the plight of *Boy Toy*. "They're just quietly making sure it doesn't get out there."

Self-censorship. It's a dirty secret that no one in the profession wants to talk about or admit practicing. Yet everyone knows some librarians bypass good books—those with literary merit or that fill a need in their collections. The reasons range from a book's sexual content and gay themes to its language and violence—and it happens in more public and K-12 libraries than you think.

"It's probably fairly widespread, but we don't have any way of really knowing, because people who self-censor are not likely to broadcast it," says Pat Scales, president of the Association for Library Service to Children and author of *Protecting Intellectual Freedom in Your School Library*. And since most people think librarians are the best champions of books, adds Scales, their jobs give them the perfect cover.

The American Library Association's (ALA) Office for Intellectual Freedom only documents written challenges to library books and materials (there were 420 cases in 2007), and even then, it estimates that only one out of five cases are reported. But when it comes to self-censorship, it's almost impossible to quantify because no one is monitoring it or collecting stats, and there's no open discussion on the subject. We most often hear about it through anecdotes or if someone is willing to fess up.

Under the Radar

"In a way, self-censorship is more frightening than outright banning and removal of challenged material," says author and former librarian Susan Patron, because these incidents tend to "slip under the radar."

The extent of the problem gained nationwide attention when Patron won the 2007 Newbery Medal, the most prestigious award in children's literature, for *The Higher Power of Lucky*. Suddenly, elementary school librarians across the country were vowing to ban her book all because of one word: *scrotum*. Was that word really appropriate in a book aimed at 9- to 12-year-olds, asked many librarians? Indeed, the subject ignited a heated debate on blogs and electronic discussion boards and thrust the issue of self-censorship onto the front page of the *New York Times*. (For the record, there have been no official challenges to *Lucky* to date.)

Reasons for Rejecting Books

Why do some librarians reject books with edgy content? In the first survey of its kind, *School Library Journal* (*SLJ*) recently asked 655 media specialists about their collections and found that 70 percent of librarians say they won't buy certain controversial titles simply because they're terrified of how parents will respond. Other common reasons for avoiding possible troublemakers include potential backlash from the administration (29 percent), the community (29 percent), or students (25 percent), followed by 23 percent of librarians who say they won't purchase a book due to personal objections.

Interestingly, nearly half of those surveyed (49 percent) say they've dealt with a book challenge. And once someone's been burned by the experience, it's hard not to let it affect future book purchases, says Joan Bertin, executive director of the National Coalition Against Censorship. Despite this, however, 80 percent say those challenges haven't affected their book-buying decisions.

Even so, Judy Blume, one of the most banned children's authors in the United States, says it's impossible to guess what will tick off censors these days. "I always tell people, 'You think you're safe? Think again, because when you're writing, anything can be seen as dangerous.'" And it's not just right-wing conservative Christians. Politically correct lefties challenge books, too. Like when a progressive mom asked that Blume's *Tales of a Fourth Grade Nothing* be removed from her daughter's class because it included a scene with a dead turtle. "She said, 'Don't you know that reptiles have feelings, and reptiles feel fear?'" Blume recalls.

Giving in to Fear

Author Rachel Vail had a similar incident late last year [2008]—but this time the censor was a librarian. After being invited to speak at an elementary school in Woodbury, NY, Vail says she was told that her latest picture book, *Jibberwillies at Night*, would be barred from the library and copies would not be available for sale in conjunction with her visit. The reason? *Jibberwillies*—which received a starred review from *Publishers Weekly* and others—deals with children's nighttime terrors and might make kids develop fears or worries that they otherwise didn't have, Vail says she was told.

"I didn't even realize it was actual censorship until after the fact," adds Vail, who was subsequently uninvited. "To have my book banned by a librarian is just shocking to me."

Some may argue that librarians are merely selecting what they feel are the best books for kids and that it's not censorship. But the key factor is one's intent. A trained media specialist is expected to choose a range of titles that best suits the curriculum and meets the reading needs of students—and that involves making judgment calls. "But if you reject a book just because of its subject matter or if you think that it would cause you some problems, then that's self-censorship," says Scales. "And that's going against professional ethics."

Censorship takes place anytime a book is removed from its intended audience, Scales adds. And it includes public libraries that move kids' books to the adult section, as well as media specialists who bowdlerize [cut parts of] books or rate

The 10 Most Challenged Books of 2008

1. *And Tango Makes Three*, by Justin Richardson and Peter Parnell

2. *His Dark Materials* (trilogy), by Philip Pullman

3. *TTYL; TTFN; L8R, G8R* (series), by Lauren Myracle

4. *Scary Stories* (series), by Alvin Schwartz

5. *Bless Me, Ultima*, by Rudolfo Anaya

6. *The Perks of Being a Wallflower*, by Stephen Chbosky

7. *Gossip Girl* (series), by Cecily von Ziegesar

8. *Uncle Bobby's Wedding*, by Sarah S. Brannen

*American Library Association,
"Frequently Challenged Books," 2009.
www.ala.org.*

them like they do movies, or who put titles in a restricted area. Other excuses librarians tend to hide behind are lack of money or shelf space. Then, of course, there's always "It doesn't fit our curriculum" or "We don't have any gay students."

Censoring "Street Lit"

Coe Booth says she knows of a few libraries in which her first novel, *Tyrell*—an ALA Best Book for Young Adults about a 15-year-old Bronx boy whose family is homeless—is in a glass display case or behind the checkout desk instead of on the shelf in the teen section. "It's definitely very frustrating—especially since it's being done in anticipation of a challenge, not in reaction to any real complaints," she says.

Even more infuriating, says Booth, is labeling. "It seems that any book with an African American character on the cover is quickly being labeled street lit, regardless of the subject matter or the setting of the book."

Meanwhile, books about Caucasian characters in urban settings don't get lumped into that genre. "It's a form of racism," she says, because the street lit category is an "easy way for some librarians to label a book that they can quickly dismiss as being inferior"—and for that reason, choose not to buy.

But racism doesn't top the list of reasons why librarians censor. They tend to be skittish about book purchases for obvious reasons. Sexual content ranks number one, with 87 percent of those surveyed by *SLJ* saying it's the main reason they shy away from buying a book. Objectionable language (61 percent) comes in second, followed by violence (51 percent), homosexual themes (47 percent), racism (34 percent), and religion (16 percent).

Censoring Gay Literature

Not surprisingly, titles with gay themes get their very own category when it comes to book banning, whether self-imposed or not, because "people have a very rigid, narrow view of what kinds of sexuality are allowed to exist," says author Jordan Sonnenblick, who's the spokesman for a group called AS IF! (Authors Support Intellectual Freedom). And oftentimes, librarians lump gay characters into the mix with sex.

Take, for example, the experience John Coy, the author of *Box Out*, had after an appearance at a suburban Minneapolis bookstore last fall. "I later found out that middle school librarians were saying they couldn't carry the book because there was one lesbian character in it—and she wasn't the main focus of the book," says Coy, who was stunned because, if anything, he had anticipated objections to the novel's questioning of school prayer.

The banning of picture books with prominent gay characters, such as *And Tango Makes Three* by Peter Parnell and Justin Richardson and *Uncle Bobby's Wedding* by Sarah S. Brannen, also makes it clear that same-sex relationships alone—not language or sexual content—are what give many people pause. Although we'll never know the level of self-censorship over these books, one 2007 study by the University of Central Arkansas shows that less than one percent of school libraries in that conservative state have books containing gay subjects or story lines—a clear sign that some heavy-duty cherry-picking is going on.

Researchers Jeff Whittingham and Wendy Rickman asked media specialists if their collections offered the most popular gay-, bisexual-, lesbian-, and transgender-themed books published between 1999 and 2005, including Alex Sanchez's *Rainbow Boys*, Brent Hartinger's *Geography Club*, and David Levithan's award-winning *Boy Meets Boy*. Almost always, the answer came back no.

Interestingly, Levithan says he intentionally wrote *Boy Meets Boy* as clean as possible so that if the book were ever challenged, the only logical reason would be because it features "happy gay characters in love." His explanation for the study's results? Librarians often let "fear, not principle, guide their choices, which is deeply unfair to the teens they serve," Levithan says.

> "For those who seek to indulge in the
> world of books, it's comforting to know
> that the religious censors are a lot less
> powerful than they once were."

Book Banning Is Declining in the United States

Rob Boston

In the following viewpoint, Rob Boston argues that religiously based book censorship has decreased in America since its heyday in the late nineteenth and early twentieth centuries. Although many books continue to face challenges in school and public libraries, he concedes, citizens can now easily obtain nearly any book they wish to read. Boston is the assistant director of communications for Americans United for Separation of Church and State, an organization that promotes freedom of religion.

As you read, consider the following questions:

1. What books did Pastor Doug Taylor censor, according to the author?

2. What books did John Sumner ban, as noted by Rob Boston?

Rob Boston, "Fanning the Flames: The 'Golden Age' of Ameican Book Burning," *Humanist*, July-August 2008, pp. 36–37. Copyright © 2008 by the American Humanist Association. Reproduced by permission of the author.

3. What is the biggest threat to books today, in the author's opinion?

On November 15, 2001, fundamentalist pastor Doug Taylor gathered his followers in a public park in Lewiston, Maine, for an old-fashioned book burning. The target of Taylor's wrath was J.K. Rowling's phenomenally successful series of Harry Potter books.

There was one problem, however: The local fire department had informed Taylor that there was no way he was going to build a bonfire on public space. Ever resourceful, the minister brandished a large pair of scissors and mutilated the book before a crowd of onlookers.

"Some of you young people should take a look at where you're going," Taylor admonished a group of children who were present. "Hell is a very bad place."

Hell, as conceived by fundamentalist Christians, sounds like a very bad place indeed. But the existence of a fiery pit filled with sadistic demons has always been debatable. The intellectual prison offered by Taylor and his ilk, however, is not. It is alive and well, and many people have chosen to enter it and slam the door behind them. Talk about a living hell!

A History of Censorship

There was a time when religious pressure groups tried to take a lot of others with them to that unhappy place. We look at the antics of Taylor and rightly feel great dismay—a man wanted to burn books in America in the twenty-first century?—but at least he didn't have the government on his side. There was a time, not so long ago, when he just might have.

Although it's not widely discussed today, the United States has a long, embarrassing history of religiously based censorship. Some books now considered classics were simply unavailable for decades due to pressure from religious communities or actions by self-appointed and legally dubious municipal boards that sought to suppress "vice."

The New York Society for the Suppression of Vice [an organization founded in 1873 and chartered by the New York state legislature], for example, never wielded any official power. It might as well have, because the organization that became infamous under Anthony Comstock had the power to suppress whatever it didn't like.

Comstock's successor, John Sumner, got especially worked up over books dealing with sex and religion (surprise!). When [American satiric novelist] Sinclair Lewis published *Elmer Gantry* in 1926, Sumner ordered Boston District Attorney William J. Foley to ban it. A year before, Sumner had engineered the suppression of [American novelist] Theodore Dreiser's *An American Tragedy*. The city of Boston, seen by today's fundamentalist Christians as a hotbed of East Coast, freethinking liberalism, was so puritanical at the time that Sumner's actions barely raised an eyebrow.

Regional Censorship Campaigns

Different denominations held sway in various regions of the country. In the South, fundamentalist Protestants were powerful, and books that mentioned the dreaded "e-word" (evolution) were verboten [forbidden] in public schools. In northern states, especially in New England and parts of the upper Midwest, the hierarchy of the Catholic Church busily acted as censors.

In 1955 church-state activist Paul Blanshard penned *The Right to Read: The Battle Against Censorship*. The book is rich with examples of religiously based censorship. In St. Cloud, Minnesota, for example, officials banned William Faulkner's *The Wild Palms*, W. Somerset Maugham's *Cakes and Ale* and other works. In Youngstown, Ohio a crusading police chief sent a letter to booksellers in town that included a list of 400 books they were instructed to stop selling, including John Steinbeck's *Cannery Row* and Ernest Hemingway's *Across the River and into the Trees*.

Changing Views of Obscenity

Early in the 20th century, works of fiction came increasingly under attack. Many books, such as James Joyce's *Ulysses* and D.H. Lawrence's *Lady Chatterley's Lover*, were banned in several countries on grounds of obscenity. Such bans produced a great deal of controversy because the "obscene" novels turned out to be, in the opinion of many literary critics, works of outstanding literary merit. Eventually, most of these bans were lifted, and the explicit depiction of sexual anatomy and sexual acts to which contemporaries objected are quite commonplace in the literature of today, indicating that what is considered obscene at one point in history will not be at another.

Nigel Barber,
"Pornography: Science, Technology, and the Law,"
Encyclopedia of Ethics in Science and Technology.
New York: Facts on File, 2002.

Perhaps unique among denominations, the Catholic Church actually published a list of forbidden books, which it updated regularly. The "Index Librorum Prohibitorum" was launched in 1557 and wasn't discontinued until 1966. Blacklisted titles included Gustave Flaubert's *Madame Bovary*, Victor Hugo's *Les Misérables*, and nonfiction works such as Edward Gibbon's *The History of the Decline and Fall of the Roman Empire*, Immanuel Kant's *Critique of Pure Reason*, and works by John Stuart Mill. Some writers, such as Honoré de Balzac, Émile Zola, and Jean-Paul Sartre, had the dubious distinction of having their entire output placed on the list.

Had the list been pitched mainly as a voluntary guide for Catholics, it probably wouldn't have captured much attention, but in some communities officials simply went after any book on it. Such was the power of the censors that when MGM movie studios made a film version of *Madame Bovary* in 1949, it had to add a prologue making it clear that the story was purely a product of Flaubert's imagination.

A Waning Trend

Such battles seem alien to many Americans today. Religiously based censorship gradually wilted under court rulings and shifting public attitudes. The last great wave of book burnings occurred during the "Red Scare" [anti-Communist crusade] of the 1950s. Prodded by the American Legion [a veterans organization], hordes of youngsters gathered up material said to promote "juvenile delinquency" and heaved it onto bonfires.

In his recent book *The Ten-Cent Plague*, David Hajdu writes about one such drive, aimed at comic books and led by Girl Scouts, in the bucolic small town of Indiana, Pennsylvania. It's nearly impossible to imagine the famous cookie sellers, celebrated for their progressive spirit and empowerment virtues, tolerating book burning today.

Books Are Readily Available

Thanks to the rise of the Internet, people can now order a book with a few mouse clicks and have it in their home within days. Web sites like Bookfinder.com and Half.com have made it possible to track down long out-of-print works. In addition, Americans have made it clear that they simply will not accept clerical interferences in their reading choices.

Of course this doesn't mean religious right censors have closed up shop. They continue to take aim at children's literature. Every year, the American Library Association compiles a list of censorship attempts. Many these days focus on tomes assigned to young people in public schools. Certain books, such as *The Catcher in the Rye* [by J.D. Salinger] and *Of Mice and Men* [by John Steinbeck], make the list with depressing regularity.

Public libraries are also under the gun, with right-wing fundamentalist pressure groups like Focus on the Family insisting that they be "family friendly"—that is, purged of books the religious right doesn't like (volumes dealing with homosexuality, Eastern religions, free thought, the "occult," and so on).

Ironically, the biggest threat to books these days may come not from religious right censors but apathetic Americans. Recent surveys have shown a precarious drop in reading for pleasure. One 2007 survey found that 25 percent of Americans had read no books during the previous twelve months. The most voracious readers were older people.

But for those who seek to indulge in the world of books, it's comforting to know that the religious censors are a lot less powerful today than they once were. If you want to read it, it is generally available—even the collected works of Honoré de Balzac.

> *"It can hardly be argued that either students or teachers shed their constitutional rights to freedom of speech or expression at the schoolhouse gate."*

Student Speech Should Not Be Censored

Debra J. Saunders

In 2002, Joseph Frederick, a high school senior, unfurled a banner saying "Bong Hits 4 Jesus" at a school event. The school's principal destroyed the banner and suspended Frederick, who in turn claimed that his First Amendment right to free speech had been violated. The case reached the Supreme Court. In the following viewpoint, Debra J. Saunders argues that the principal did in fact violate Frederick's rights and that ruling against him would threaten all students' right to free speech. Saunders is a conservative columnist for the San Francisco Chronicle *newspaper.*

Editor's Note: In 2007, the Supreme Court ruled against Frederick.

Debra J. Saunders, "Schoolhouse Prankster at the Gate," *San Francisco Chronicle*, March 20, 2007, p. B7. Copyright © 2007 San Francisco Chronicle. Reproduced by permission of the author.

As you read, consider the following questions:

1. What "strange bedfellow" coalition united in support of Joseph Frederick, according to the author?

2. What examples does Judge Andrew Kleinfeld give of texts that could be deemed disruptive under the Court's precedent in the Frederick case, as quoted by Debra J. Saunders?

3. Why is the principal most at fault in the *Frederick* case, in the author's opinion?

Every group in power has its fervent rationale for believing that it has a right, even a duty, to suppress speech it doesn't like. That's why America has a Supreme Court—to slap some sense into the censorious.

Yesterday [March 19, 2007], lawyers argued a case that should have been settled years ago. It began in January 2002. As an Alaska high school released students so that they could attend a "Winter Olympics Torch Relay," then 18-year-old senior Joseph Frederick unfurled a banner that read, "Bong Hits 4 Jesus" from a Juneau sidewalk. Frederick thought the nonsensical message would get him on TV.

And it did—Frederick's name was broadcast across America, thanks to his high school principal, Deborah Morse. Morse saw the banner, crossed the street and tore it up. She also suspended Frederick for 10 days.

Frederick appealed to the school board and lost. He went to court, where a federal judge ruled against him. But in 2006, the Ninth U.S. Circuit Court of Appeals ruled 3-0 for Frederick.

A Dangerous Argument

Now the case is before the Big Bench. [The Supreme Court ruled against Frederick in June 2007]. Leaders of the religious right, who want to protect the free speech rights of religious

Students Are Entitled to Freedom of Expression

In our system, state-operated schools may not be enclaves of totalitarianism. School officials do not possess absolute authority over their students. Students in school as well as out of school are "persons" under our Constitution. They are possessed of fundamental rights which the State must respect, just as they themselves must respect their obligations to the State. In our system, students may not be regarded as closed-circuit recipients of only that which the State chooses to communicate. They may not be confined to the expression of those sentiments that are officially approved. In the absence of a specific showing of constitutionally valid reasons to regulate their speech, students are entitled to freedom of expression of their views.

Abraham Fortas, U.S. Supreme Court:
Tinker v. Des Moines School District, *393 U.S. 503 (1969).*

students, have joined with drug-war dissidents, like the group Students for Sensible Drug Policy [SSDP], whose members protested outside the Supreme Court building. Eric Sterling, an SSDP board member, told me this is not the first time he has been involved in "strange bedfellow" coalitions in which one group sees "the infringement of the civil liberties" of a group as likely to affect all.

On the school board's side stand the [George W.] Bush administration and former special prosecutor Ken Starr, who has come up with a scary argument in support of Frederick's suspension. Starr told the justices that schools should be able to silence students if their speech disrupts "the educational mission of the school."

Follow the logic. Juneau schools tell kids to stay away from drugs. If students argue—or even joke—they are being, in Starr's words, "disruptive."

The Ninth Circuit understood how this precedent could be used to punish freethinking teens. Judge Andrew Kleinfeld wrote, "All sorts of missions are undermined by legitimate and protected speech—a school's anti-gun mission would be undermined by a student passing around copies of John R. Lott's book, *More Guns, Less Crime*, a school's anti-alcohol mission would be undermined by a student e-mailing links to a medical study showing less heart disease among moderate drinkers than teetotalers."

Sterling predicted that the Supremes will "both uphold and reverse" the Ninth Circuit ruling, by agreeing that the suspension was a violation of Frederick's rights, but reversing the finding that Morse could be held personally liable for damages.

The Big Bench must not walk away from a 1969 ruling [*Tinker v. Des Moines*] that upheld students' rights to wear black armbands to protest the Vietnam War, noting, "it can hardly be argued that either students or teachers shed their constitutional rights to freedom of speech or expression at the schoolhouse gate."

David Crosby, an attorney who represented Juneau schools early on, complained to the *Anchorage Daily News* that the "carefully manipulated image of Joe Frederick as a latter-day Thoreau"[1] is "offensive and ludicrous."

Crosby has a point. Frederick won't even admit that "Bong Hits 4 Jesus" was a pro-marijuana message. Also, as the *Anchorage Daily News* reported, Frederick pleaded guilty to misdemeanor sale of marijuana in 2004.

But if anyone has made Frederick into a civil-disobedience hero, it is Morse, who went overboard punishing a smart-

---

1. Henry David Thoreau was an American author and philosopher known for his theory of social change via civil disobedience.

aleck kid. At first, she suspended Frederick for five days. Then, she upped it to 10 days—she says, because he would not name his accomplices, he says, because he quoted Thomas Jefferson on free speech.

She could have tried to reason with the kid. Or she could have used adults' most potent weapon—ignoring him. Instead, Morse gave the smart mouth the grounds to turn a prank into a federal case.

> *"Students will test the limits of acceptable behavior in myriad ways . . . ; school officials need a degree of flexible authority to respond to disciplinary challenges."*

Student Speech Should Be Censored

Daniel Henninger

In the following viewpoint, Daniel Henninger, deputy editor of the Wall Street Journal's *editorial page, applauds a 2007 Supreme Court decision giving schools the right to discipline students for promoting illegal drug use. He contends that the ruling is one step toward restoring public schools to their traditional role as places that promote socially acceptable values and behaviors.*

As you read, consider the following questions:

1. What was the premise of Justice Clarence Thomas's concurring opinion in the *Morse v. Frederick* case, according to the author?

Daniel Henninger, "Wonder Land: Bong Hits 4 Jesus—Final Episode," *Wall Street Journal,* June 28, 2007, p. A12. Copyright © 2007 by Dow Jones & Company. Republished with permission of Wall Street Journal, conveyed through Copyright Clearance Center, Inc.

2. How does Daniel Henninger account for the increase in the number of parents turning to homeschooling, parochial schools, private schools, and charter schools for their children?

3. What has been the result of the 1969 *Tinker v. Des Moines* decision, in the author's opinion?

Maybe I should have gone to law school. But only if God promised I would grow up to be a justice on the Supreme Court. The Nine Interpreters may have more fun than anyone in public life. Tip the United States on its side and eventually everything loose rolls into the Supreme Court. Justice Antonin Scalia, a skilled ironist, by now treats the Court's annual agenda like a man at a driving range with a bucket of golf balls. What fun.

The United States began as a complex country—thus the genius of the Founders' template Constitution—and now finds itself in an infinitely complex era. The solution of we moderns to this inexorable multiplier effect has been to burden our institutions with more laws and more lawsuits. The inevitable result is a society steeped in unintended consequences. Ask the principal of a public high school.

The Background of the *Morse* Case

You have guessed by now that we are going to discuss the famous case known as "Bong Hits 4 Jesus," aka *Morse v. Frederick*, decided by the Supreme Court this past Monday [June 25, 2007]. Juneau, Alaska, high school principal Deborah Morse defeated high school troublemaker Joseph Frederick in a split decision, 5–4.

Years back, as the Olympic Torch parade passed by her Alaskan high school, Principal Morse ran across the street from the school's front door and ordered student Frederick to lower his "Bong Hits 4 Jesus" banner, judging it a violation of the school district's anti-drug policy. A "bong" is a marijuana water pipe. A "hit" is the extraction of marijuana smoke from the bong. The meaning of "4 Jesus" remains in dispute. Mr. Frederick demanded his constitutional rights. On Monday [June 25, 2007], the High Court said, not this time.

The *Morse* Decision

It is no exaggeration to say the basis for the decision was akin to passing a camel through the eye of a needle. For space reasons, I will briefly "interpret" Chief Justice [John] Roberts's ruling. What he said is that the list of things the Constitution forbids a child to say in our public schools is very short. You can say almost anything. But as of Monday [June 25, 2007], the list is a little longer: You can't engage in speech "promoting illegal drug use." Hereafter, speech "promoting illegal drug use" may be regarded as "disruptive" to school life, as defined by the Supreme Court in *Tinker* [*v. Des Moines*] (1969), [*Bethel School District v.*] *Fraser* (1986) and [*Hazelwood v.*] *Kuhlmeier* (1988).

Justice Roberts was at pains to make clear that speech promoting "illegal drug use" is the only thing this decision proscribes. That wasn't narrow enough for the Court's other new [George W.] Bush nominee, Samuel Alito. He called it a "dangerous fiction" to "pretend" that parents hand over to school administrators the authority for what their children may say or hear. The only speech he'd forbid is that which threatens "the physical safety of students." Drug promotion qualifies. He ended by warning that *Morse* "does not endorse any further extensions" of speech limits.

Two quick thoughts: What the majority did is use the "Bong" case to throw what weight it could muster behind school authorities beset with drugged-out students and pushers. Fine. But those confirmation-hearing wails about Messrs. Roberts and Alito "overthrowing" *Roe v. Wade* [the 1973 Supreme Court decision legalizing abortion]? Not likely, so long as *Roe* qualifies as a precedent.

Freedom of Speech Does Not Apply to Students

In light of the history of American public education, it cannot seriously be suggested that the First Amendment "freedom of speech" encompasses a student's right to speak in public schools. Early public schools gave total control to teachers, who expected obedience and respect from students. And courts routinely deferred to schools' authority to make rules and to discipline students for violating those rules. Several points are clear: (1) under *in loco parentis* [in place of parents], speech rules and other school rules were treated identically; (2) the *in loco parentis* doctrine imposed almost no limits on the types of rules that a school could set while students were in school; and (3) schools and teachers had tremendous discretion in imposing punishments for violations of those rules.

Clarence Thomas,
U.S. Supreme Court: Concurring Opinion,
Deborah Morse v. Joseph Frederick, *June 25, 2007.*

The State of Public Schools

Meanwhile, Justice Clarence Thomas, in a concurring opinion, took about half a line to say, "I agree," and proceeded to write one of the most compelling essays I've seen on the decline and fall of American public education. I would happily hand out Justice Thomas's opinion on street corners (though www.supremecourtus.gov relieves me of that burden).

What he's done is rummage back through school cases, mostly from 19th century state courts, to invoke the idea of a public school. His premise is that the schools' role was most certainly *in loco parentis* [in place of parents], in that they and parents broadly agreed on what made an adolescent grow into a good person; what schools need least is court interference in this hard job.

A North Carolina court in 1837 spoke of the need "to control stubbornness, to quicken diligence and to reform bad habits." In 1886, a Maine court said school leaders must "quicken the slothful, spur the indolent and restrain the impetuous." An 1859 Vermont court spoke of preserving "decency and decorum."

Missouri's court in 1885 found reasonable a rule that "forbade the use of profane language." Indiana's in 1888 ruled in favor of "good deportment." An 1843 manual for schoolmasters speaks of "a core of common values" and teaching the "power of self-control, and a habit of postponing present indulgence to a greater future good."

Getting Back to the Three Ds

Antique words from a world long gone? Even Justice Thomas admits "the idea of treating children as though it were the 19th century would find little support today." I'm not so sure about that. How else can one explain the flight from the public schools—into homeschooling, parochial schools, private schools and even charter schools, which invest public principals with greater control? Parents are spending thousands to have what American schools had from 1859 to 1959—some basic measure of the Three Ds: decorum, decency and diligence. Self-control as a higher "common value" than out-of-control.

Justice Thomas argues that the 1969 *Tinker* case dragged the schools into a morass of arcane First Amendment jurisprudence. He's right.

Here's a final quotation from Monday's [June 25, 2007] "Bong" decision to pass out on street corners: "Students will test the limits of acceptable behavior in myriad ways better known to schoolteachers than to judges; school officials need a degree of flexible authority to respond to disciplinary challenges; and the law has always considered the relationship between teachers and students special. Under these circumstances, the more detailed the Court's supervision becomes, the more likely its law will engender further disputes among teachers and students. Consequently, larger numbers of those disputes will likely make their way from the schoolhouse to the courthouse. Yet no one wishes to substitute courts for school boards, or to turn the judge's chambers into the principal's office." More right-wing rant from Clarence Thomas? Nope, that's liberal Justice Stephen Breyer's concurrence.

I'll go further. Because of the *Tinker* case in 1969, much of the cultural disarray of the past 35 years flowed out of schools and into society. Teachers today will tell you their discipline problems start at home. *Tinker* should be tossed. Once the schools can again help people learn the value of a relatively orderly life and self-control, the rest would follow.

> "The only way to effectively desecrate the American flag would be to under-cut the freedom for which it stands."

The Proposed Flag Desecration Amendment Is a Threat to Freedom

Nat Hentoff

Various veterans groups and politicians advocate a constitutional amendment criminalizing the desecration of the American flag. Opponents insist that desecration of the flag is a form of political speech and that banning the act would therefore violate the First Amendment. In the following viewpoint, Nat Hentoff, a colum-nist for the Washington Times, *opposes one such amendment: Senate Joint Resolution (S.J. Res.) 12. While he does not condone burning the flag, he insists that preserving the freedom to do so is more important than altering the Constitution to limit free-dom of expression. Following the writing of this viewpoint, SJR 12 failed to pass.*

Nat Hentoff, "Congressional Hypocrisy and Old Glory," *Washington Times*, May 29, 2006, p. A19 OPED. Copyright © Washington Times Library, May 29, 2006. Reproduced by permission.

As you read, consider the following questions:

1. What is the foundation of people's liberties, according to Senator Robert Byrd, as quoted by the author?

2. How did James Warner use a photograph of a burning American flag against his captors in Vietnam, according to Hentoff?

3. What countries currently punish the desecration of their flags, as reported by the author?

For the first time since 1791, when the Bill of Rights was ratified and added to the Constitution, Congress appears about to pass a constitutional amendment—not just a law—to the First Amendment, from which all our liberties flow. The Flag Desecration Amendment (S.J.R. 12) empowers Congress to prohibit any "physical desecration" of the American flag. I know there is a serious national deficiency in the education of our young on the Bill of Rights and the rest of the Constitution, but will Congress actually dishonor the First Amendment?

Last year [2005], the House passed this desecration of the First Amendment by an eight-vote margin. And on May 4 [2006], by a 6-3 vote, the Senate Judiciary Subcommittee on the Constitution also placed the First Amendment in jeopardy. If approved by the full Judiciary Committee, it may be that only one or two votes on the Senate floor will keep the First Amendment intact. Otherwise, President [George W.] Bush will surely sign it while declaring his devotion to our values.

The day before Flag Day last year [2005], the *Houston Chronicle* underlined what we will lose if this amendment becomes law: "It makes no sense to set fire to the Bill of Rights to prevent a few people from protesting in a way that many find offensive. The right to speak our minds in public and engage in protest is at the core of our system of government. The only way to effectively desecrate the American flag would be to undercut the freedom for which it stands." And Sen. Robert Byrd, who carries the Constitution in his DNA, speaks for James Madison across the centuries: "In the final analysis, it is the Constitution—not the flag—that is the foundation and guarantor of the people's liberties."

Among the many veterans opposing the Flag Desecration Amendment is Gary May, who lost both legs in Vietnam while serving with K Company, 3rd Battalion, 27 Marines. Last year, he said: "This amendment would not honor veterans; it would attack the very principles that inspired us to serve our country ... We fought for a society free of repression and filled with open debate." This year, on May 6 [2006], Mr. May added: "I did not lose my legs, and nearly my life, to protect a symbol." Of all the personal stories by veterans against this attempt to change the Constitution to limit open debate in this country, the most powerful was by James Warner, who, during a previous debate, told of his imprisonment by the North Vietnamese from 1967 to 1973 after volunteering for duty there and flying more than 100 missions before being shot down. Refusing to accede to his captors' offer to be released if he admitted this country had been wrong in Vietnam, Mr. Warner was tortured and spent 13 months in solitary confinement.

During one interrogation, an enemy officer gleefully showed Mr. Warner a photograph of Americans protesting the war by burning the flag.

"There," the officer crowed, "people in your country protest against your cause! That proves you are wrong!" If only Congress and the president would listen to Mr. Warner's answer to the rejoicing jailer: "No. That (photograph) proves I am right. In my country, we are not afraid of freedom, even if it means that people disagree with us. The officer was on his feet in an instant, his face purple with rage. He smashed his fist on the table and screamed at me to shut up. While he was ranting, I was astonished to see pain, confounded by fear, in his eyes. I have never forgotten that look, nor have I forgotten

Used with permission of Signe Wilkinson and the Washington Post Writers Group in conjunction with the Cartoonist Group. All rights reserved.

the satisfaction I felt at using his tool—the picture of a burning flag—against him." The much-decorated Mr. Warner went on to serve in the White House as a domestic policy adviser to President [Ronald] Reagan during his second term, and is a recently retired corporate attorney. He will be one of the speakers on June 6 [2006] at a debate on the Flag Desecration Amendment in the aptly named First Amendment Room in the National Press Club in Washington.

Paul McMasters, First Amendment ombudsman at the First Amendment Center, will be the moderator with debaters attorney Robert Corn-Revere (against) and Adrian Cronauer (for)—the latter is national director of the Citizens Flag Alliance.

During the Vietnam War, my wife and I protested against it, but when we saw antiwar activists burning the flag in protest, we bought a flag and flew it outside our home to show those burning Old Glory that they utterly failed to understand that the flag speaks for the right of all Americans to speak freely. The year before, an angry Vietnam War veteran was once about to punch me on the nose for opposing the amendment until I quickly asked him: "What does the flag mean to you?" He paused. "Liberty!" he shouted, and walked away. That dimension of our liberty may soon disappear because, if the amendment becomes law all 50 state legislatures have already endorsed resolutions in favor of this amendment.

The only countries I know that punish the desecration of their flags are China, Iran and Cuba.

Do we want to join those dictatorships?

> "Burning the flag is not a form of con-
> structive speech but an act of physical
> assault."

The Proposed Flag Desecration Amendment Is Not a Threat to Freedom

Bill Frist

Bill Frist is a physician and businessman who served in the U.S. Senate from 1995 to 2007. In the following viewpoint, Frist argues that burning the American flag is not a form of legitimate political speech, but rather an act of vandalism. Therefore, he supports a constitutional amendment to make flag desecration illegal. The American flag is a symbol of the nation's unity, strength, and ideals, Frist insists, and thus deserves to be enshrined by law.

As you read, consider the following questions:

1. What historical examples does the author cite to illustrate how important the American flag is?

2. What percentage of Americans support a flag desecration amendment, according to Bill Frist?

Bill Frist, "Why We Must Protect the American Flag," Human Events.com, March 14, 2006. Copyright © 2006 Human Events Inc. Reproduced by permission.

3. What criminal act does the author compare flag desecration to?

Americans have much to be proud of. We enjoy a greater measure of liberty, justice, and equality than any other country throughout history. There is one symbol that, above all others, encapsulates the history and values we hold dear: the American flag. From the time we're schoolchildren, we honor our flag and all it stands for with hand over heart and a deep appreciation for the blessings we enjoy as Americans.

In times of crisis, the raising of the Stars and Stripes symbolizes perseverance and enduring strength. Whether it's Marines struggling to plant the flag on Iwo Jima [a Japanese island that was the site of a major battle in World War II] or firefighters lifting the flag above the ruins of the World Trade Center [site of the September 11, 2001 terrorist attacks], patriotic Americans have always taken heart in knowing that "our flag was still there."

Enemies of American freedom abroad are well aware of the ideals emblemized by the American flag, often expressing anti-American sentiments by burning our flag. Unfortunately, almost 20 years ago the Supreme Court essentially ruled in favor of allowing flag burning here at home. In a 1989 decision that overturned 200 years of precedent, the court struck down all laws that prohibit flag desecration.

An Amendment Is Needed

The vast majority of Americans—80 percent—and all 50 of our state legislatures believe the flag should be protected. Given the misguided Supreme Court ruling, the only way we can protect the flag is through amending the Constitution.

Before Congress adjourns to celebrate the Fourth of July this year [2006], I intend to bring the Flag Protection Amendment to the floor. The proposed amendment is a simple, one-sentence statement that reads: "The Congress shall have the

Not an Absolute Right

Freedom of speech is not an absolute right. Certainly there are occasions where speech is restricted; the most simplistic example is the prohibition against yelling "fire!" in a crowded theater. But other forms of speech have also been outlawed. Certain forms of obscenity, threats and libel are forms of speech which have been banned. Hate speech is another form of illegal speech. Hate speech can be very vague and subject to interpretation. The flag is a unique, identifiable symbol. Protecting this specific symbol is actually less restrictive than banning language which may be construed as "hate speech."

Joseph Petrocelli,
"Should Flag Burning Be Prohibited?
It's Not as Simple as You Might Think,"
Officer.com, July 8, 2008. www.officer.com.

power to prohibit the physical desecration of the flag of the United States." [Editor's note: The amendment failed to pass.]

As Harvard Law professor Richard Parker explains: "The amendment process is essential to the Constitution's deepest foundation—the principle of popular sovereignty affirmed in its first words, 'We the people.' Making use of this process reaffirms and thus preserves that foundation."

Flag Burning Is Not Speech

Opponents of the measure claim flag burning should be protected as an exercise of free speech. To these individuals, I would ask: Is defacing a government building speech? No, it is considered a criminal act of vandalism. By the same token, burning the flag is not a form of constructive speech but an act of physical assault. America is the freest country in the world, and its citizens have the right to express dissent in myriad ways. Exercising one's right to free speech by destroying the very icon of that right need not be one of them.

We pledge our allegiance to the flag with the words "one nation, under God." But burning the flag is a deeply divisive act that shows contempt for all that unites us as Americans.

The Constitution itself supplies the appropriate remedy through the amendment process, and I believe it is fitting to use that process to restore the ability of Congress to protect the flag that countless brave men and women have died defending.

I look forward to debating the Flag Protection Amendment on the Senate floor. And I am hopeful that Congress will support the wishes of the majority of American citizens by voting to protect this noble symbol of our common heritage.

> *"Forcing [radio] stations to operate ...*
> *in an ideological and multicultural*
> *affirmative-action system that dictates*
> *'fairness' ... is unconstitutional."*

Regulation of Talk Radio Will Threaten Free Speech

Alan Sears

From 1949 to 1987, the Federal Communications Commission's "Fairness Doctrine" imposed talk show content requirements on broadcasters. In recent years, some commentators have advocated resurrecting this policy to counter the popularity of conservative talk shows on the radio. In the following viewpoint, Alan Sears opposes this effort. He contends that rather than to bring balance to the airwaves, the return of the "Fairness Doctrine" is designed to squelch conservative talk radio. Sears is a conservative columnist and the president, CEO, and general counsel of the Alliance Defense Fund (ADF), a Christian legal alliance defending religious liberty, sanctity of life, marriage, and the family.

As you read, consider the following questions:

1. In a free market, who decides which radio programs live and die, according to the author?

Alan Sears, "'Fairness Doctrine' Is a Code Name for 'Censorship,'" Townhall.com, June 26, 2007. Reproduced by permission of the author.

2. Why is regulation such as the Fairness Doctrine irrelevant in today's media climate, in Alan Sears's opinion?

3. How did the Fairness Doctrine discourage free speech when it was in effect, according to the author?

Leftist censors aren't just dropping hints about their determination to legislate conservative talk radio out of existence. They are screaming their intentions, loud and clear.

In the wake of the pending final demise of bankrupt and scandal-plagued Air America, the Left continues to be frustrated by the fact that America simply isn't tuning in to their propaganda. So, according to reports from various news outlets, House Speaker Nancy Pelosi, Rep. Steny Hoyer, Dennis Kucinich, and Sen. Dianne Feinstein are joining their friends at the far-Left Center for American Progress [CAP] to cook up a new plan: force radio stations to accept unwanted programming in the name of "fairness" and "balance."

Speaker Pelosi has reportedly promised to "aggressively pursue" revival of the poorly titled "Fairness Doctrine," whose regulations would mandate that radio stations featuring the views of conservatives like Michael Medved, Hugh Hewitt, or Bill O'Reilly "balance" those views (in the name of diversity) with an "equal" dose of, say, Al Franken, Randi Rhodes, or Thom Hartmann—all proven failures in a free radio market.

As if that news wasn't alarming enough, a report released by CAP last week added even more fuel to the fire, reminding conservatives just how far the Left-wing will go to silence dissent.

The organization's report, titled "The Structural Imbalance of Political Talk Radio," expresses a need to "close the gap" between conservative and Left-wing programming. It also advocates increasing "ownership diversity, both in terms of the race/ethnicity and gender of owners, as well as the number of independent local owners," which in the Left's view would lead to more "diverse" programs. So instead of capitalism, we get the Leftist cure-all: quotas.

In a free market, the listeners decide which radio programs live and which die. Forcing stations to operate not on the basis of ratings and ad revenue, but in an ideological and multicultural affirmative-action system that dictates "fairness," is not only unconstitutional—it's downright Soviet. It's offensive to the economic marketplace; it's suffocating to the vital marketplace of ideas.

But, of course, that persnickety First Amendment has never stopped the Left before. They're more than happy to rewrite it and bully Americans into submission, if they can't capture and sustain an audience the old-fashioned way.

When the Fairness Doctrine was first introduced in 1949, it required licensed broadcasters to devote equal time to both sides of a controversial issue, and mandated that stations air programming addressing issues of local interest. At a time when television was in its infancy, satellite radio a fantasy, and the Internet non-existent, such rules may have had some merit. But in today's market, with hundreds of choices in programming, such regulations are irrelevant—and nearly impossible to enforce.

But the Fairness Doctrine is more than useless—it's counterproductive. The FCC realized 20 years ago that the law actually discouraged, rather than encouraged, more free speech. Rather than try to gauge what legally constituted "equal time" for both sides of a political contest, station owners began just dropping politically-based programming altogether. That led to the FCC's ending enforcement of the doctrine in 1987.

The fact is that the success of conservative talk radio is a direct response to the Left's virtual 50-year stranglehold on American media through its domination of all the major network and cable television outlets . . . through public broadcasting stations such as PBS and NPR . . . and through virtually every major American newspaper. Conservatives are simply fed up with Left-wing bias, and their heartfelt embrace of talk radio is clear evidence of their outrage.

It's time for the Left to cut the static: Behind the calls for "regulation" and "diversity" hides a posse of political bullies who realize that they cannot compete against the likes of Sean Hannity or Rush Limbaugh in a free market. The Left-wing's failure to capture anything beyond a tiny niche market isn't the fault of the FCC, nor of the dormant Fairness Doctrine. The "blame" rests with radio listeners who came, listened, and chose to tune out of "Dead Air" America.

> *"We want either clear rules that pro-*
> *mote . . . First Amendment values or a*
> *reasonable payment to the public for*
> *the use of its property."*

Regulation of Talk Radio Will Protect Free Speech

Mark Lloyd

In the following viewpoint, Mark Lloyd argues that political talk radio is dominated by conservative programming due to biased media owners who refuse to broadcast liberal programs. In response, Lloyd does not advocate a return to the Fairness Doctrine—a former government policy that required broadcasters to present controversial issues in a balanced manner. Instead, he favors regulations to increase ownership opportunities for diverse peoples and require more speech that reflects the varied interests of local communities. Lloyd is vice president for strategic initiatives at the Leadership Conference on Civil Rights (LCCR), a coalition of civil rights organizations.

As you read, consider the following questions:

1. What examples does Mark Lloyd cite to demonstrate the failure of the Fairness Doctrine?

Mark Lloyd, "Forget the Fairness Doctrine," Center for American Progress, July 24, 2007. Copyright © Center for American Progress. This material was created by the *Center for American Progress*, www.americanprogress.org. Reproduced by permission.

2. What resulted in the rise of Rush Limbaugh and other conservative talk show hosts, according to the author?

3. What public interest are broadcasters required to serve, as explained by Lloyd?

The Center for American Progress late last month published a widely read report titled "The Structural Imbalance of Political Talk Radio." That report demonstrated the failure of the supposed "free market" regulation of the U.S. radio industry to address the public-interest needs of listeners. Our analysis revealed that conservative talk radio dominates the airwaves of our country—to the detriment of informed public discourse and the First Amendment.

Only the most misinformed still believe that radio group owners such as Citadel Broadcasting Corp., which refuses to air popular progressive hosts like Ed Schultz, are only concerned about the bottom line. Few would agree that markets such as Philadelphia and Houston are well-served with 100 percent conservative talk radio. But that doesn't mean that the answer to this pervasive imbalance is the Fairness Doctrine.

In our report, we call for ownership rules that we think will create greater local diversity of programming, news, and commentary. And we call for more localism by putting teeth into the licensing rules. But we do not call for a return to the Fairness Doctrine.

Despite what we thought was fairly stark evidence of conservative bias, despite clear proposals to address that bias, Rush Limbaugh and other distortionists insisted that we were calling for a "return" of the Fairness Doctrine. But as we wrote, "simply reinstating the Fairness Doctrine will do little to address the gap between conservative and progressive talk unless the underlying elements of the public trustee doctrine are enforced, in particular, the requirements of local accountability and the reasonable airing of important matters."

The power of right-wing talk radio and their echo chambers in the conservative blogosphere and Fox News was amply demonstrated by their simple "black or white, for or against" reaction to our report. They refused to discuss the underlying market control exercised by radio corporations eager to promote the conservative agenda. But it worked. Even the radio hosts of supposedly liberal public radio stations asked the authors of the report over and over, "Why are you calling for a return of the Fairness Doctrine?"

On one station, I responded that our report focused on media consolidation and localism, not the Fairness Doctrine. This sparked the host to ask, "Well, why *aren't* you calling for a return of the Fairness Doctrine?"

Okay, so why aren't we calling for a return of the Fairness Doctrine? As we state in the report, the Fairness Doctrine never by itself fostered coverage of important issues in a way that spoke to the diversity of interests in local communities across our country. In the late 1960s, the supposed golden age of the Fairness Doctrine, the Kerner Commission reported the failure of mainstream media to report on minority communities. The same could be said at the time regarding the reporting of the views of women or poor people or young people protesting against the war in Vietnam.

Despite the distortions of the Nixon-era media haters, mainstream broadcast media in the late 1960s was middleclass, anti-Communist, Protestant, male and white. If dittoheads like to think of this as a "liberal" bias, so be it, but the Fairness Doctrine didn't do much to address it.

Here's the history that matters. In the late 1960s the United Church of Christ successfully challenged the Federal Communications Commission over the lack of local input in FCC decisions. A moderate Republican judge, Warren Burger, whom Nixon later appointed as Chief Justice of the Supreme Court, sided with the church group. As a result of that ruling, a whole slew of rules were put in place to give local communities power in the licensing of broadcasters.

Misconceptions About the Fairness Doctrine

There are many misconceptions about the Fairness Doctrine. For instance, it did not require that each program be internally balanced, nor did it mandate equal time for opposing points of view. And it didn't require that the balance of a station's program lineup be anything like 50/50.

Nor, as [conservative radio host] Rush Limbaugh has repeatedly claimed, was the Fairness Doctrine all that stood between conservative talk show hosts and the dominance they would attain after the doctrine's repeal. In fact, not one Fairness Doctrine decision issued by the Federal Communications Commission (FCC) had ever concerned itself with talk shows. Indeed, the talk show format was born and flourished while the doctrine was in operation. Before the doctrine was repealed, right-wing hosts frequently dominated talk show schedules, even in liberal cities, but none was ever muzzled. The Fairness Doctrine simply prohibited stations from broadcasting from a single perspective, day after day, without presenting opposing views.

Steve Rendall, "The Fairness Doctrine:
How We Lost It, and Why We Need It Back,"
Extra! *January-February 2005.*

In their engagement in the licensing process many of those groups cited the responsibility of the broadcaster to "afford reasonable opportunity for the discussion of conflicting views of issues of public importance." This responsibility, which many think of as the core of the Fairness Doctrine, was established in the 1920s. But with public engagement in the 1970s the Fairness Doctrine finally had some teeth.

All reports of its demise to the contrary, this core responsibility remains in the Communications Act today. Today, however, the act once again simply has no teeth.

How broadcast licensees meet their responsibility of fair discussion of important public issues has varied considerably over 80 years of federal regulation. But the image of eager federal bureaucrats peering over the shoulders of all of America's radio talk show hosts with a stopwatch in hand is as absurd as it is impractical.

We trace the rise and influence of Rush and other conservative radio hosts to relaxed ownership rules and other pro-big business regulation that destroyed localism. The supposed "repeal" of the Fairness Doctrine did not create Rush Limbaugh, just as the supposedly onerous Fairness Doctrine did not destroy Joe Pyne in the 1960s or Father Charles Coughlin in the decades before Pyne.

To be fair, even some progressives are confused about the Fairness Doctrine. A recent news story reported that the League of United Latin American Citizens, or LULAC for short, has asked Speaker of the House Nancy Pelosi (D-CA) to reintroduce the Fairness Doctrine—even as the same article reports on a speech to LULAC by ABC News correspondent John Quiñones, who spoke of his work bringing to audiences a hard-earned perspective to the long-running immigration debate.

Quiñones told the LULAC audience that he got his start because a San Antonio community organization threatened that if the stations didn't hire more Latinos, the group would go to the FCC and challenge their licenses. "Thank God for them," Quiñones said. "I wouldn't be here."

Equal opportunity employment policies. Local engagement. License challenges. Nothing in there about the Fairness Doctrine.

The other part of our proposal that gets the dittoheads upset is our suggestion that the commercial radio station owners either play by the rules or pay. In other words, if they don't want to be subject to local criticism of how they are meeting their license obligations, they should pay to support public broadcasters who will operate on behalf of the local community. Commercial broadcasters want to be trustees of public property but without responsibility.

Unlike newspapers and movies and blogs and cable channels, the federal government gives commercial broadcasters a free license to use public property—the airwaves. There are still more people who want these licenses than the government is able to satisfy. In exchange for this very valuable and scarce license, and federal protection against "pirate" (unlicensed) radio operators, broadcasters are supposed to operate in the public interest.

That's the deal. The broadcasters like the free license and the free protection, but they just don't want the public involved in telling them whether they are actually serving the public interest. For 80 years the public interest has been defined as, you guessed it, providing a reasonable opportunity for the diverse expression of issues of local importance.

For over 25 years Henry Geller, a distinguished telecommunications attorney, has argued that broadcasters ignore the local public interest, that the whole "public trustee" idea is broken, and that instead of trying to make broadcasters play by the rules we should just make them pay a reasonable fee to support public broadcasting. But spectrum license fees should not be put in the federal treasury as they are now. Instead, they should be used to advance the public's First Amendment interest in diverse speech at the local and national levels. We think Geller makes a strong argument.

We at the Center are delighted at the increased attention our report has brought to the obligations of broadcasters to provide local communities they are licensed to serve with opportunities for diverse expression of important issues. The status quo does not serve our democracy well. We want to create more ownership opportunities and more speech focused on local interests. We want either clear rules that promote these First Amendment values or a reasonable payment to the public for the use of its property.

All of these public policy objectives are there for Congress and the FCC to act upon within current law. There is no need to return to the Fairness Doctrine.

Periodical Bibliography

The following articles have been selected to supplement the diverse views presented in this chapter.

L. Brent Bozell III	"Librarians Against Censorship?" Townhall.com, May 9, 2008. www.townhall.com.
Horace Cooper	"Freedom to Speak," *Washington Times*, December 5, 2008.
Nat Hentoff	"Saving Free Speech and Jesus," *Village Voice*, April 3, 2007.
Richard Just	"Unmuzzling High School Journalists," *Washington Post*, January 12, 2008.
Frank D. LoMonte	"Student Journalism Confronts a New Generation of Legal Challenges," *Human Rights*, Summer 2008.
James Miller III	"The Censorship Doctrine," *Washington Times*, November 6, 2008.
James Rainey	"Right-Wing Radio Sounds False Alarm on 'Fairness Doctrine,'" *Los Angeles Times*, November 14, 2008.
Debra J. Saunders	"Freedom of Expression Takes a Bong Hit," Townhall.com, June 27, 2007. www.townhall.com.
Gary Sawyer	"Banning Books Isn't the Answer," *Herald & Review*, October 7, 2007.
J. Peder Zane	"Good Reasons to Rebel," *News & Observer*, March 29, 2009.

For Further Discussion

Chapter 1

1. Tony Blankley argues that the media are too quick to report sensitive information about government operations. Dean Baquet and Bill Keller insist that their newspapers carefully consider the national security risks posed by each story they publish. Based on these arguments, do you believe the media are too cavalier with government secrets, too compliant with government attempts to censor them, or effective at balancing the public's right to know with the government's need for secrecy? Defend your answer with quotes from the viewpoints.

2. Do you believe the arts should be censored? If not, why not? If so, which of the following types of content should be banned: obscenity, nudity, graphic depictions of sex, anti-religious messages? Explain your rationale for your position.

3. After reading the viewpoints by Haroon Siddiqui and Flemming Rose, do you think *Jyllands-Posten* should have published the cartoons depicting the Islamic prophet Muhammad? Why or why not? Support your answer with references to the viewpoints.

Chapter 2

1. Jacob Sullum is the senior editor for *Reason*, a magazine that promotes libertarianism, a belief in limited government control over the economy and personal behavior. Does knowing his background influence your assessment of his argument against Internet pornography laws? Explain your answer.

2. After reading the viewpoints by Cesar Conda, Damian

Kulash, and Phil Kerpen, what is your view on net neutrality laws? Will they harm families, as Conda argues; protect free speech on the Internet, as Kulash insists; or lead to government control of content, as Kerpen maintains? Support your answer with references to the viewpoints.

Chapter 3

1. Based on the viewpoints by Adam B. Kushner, Richard Seymour, James Fallows, and April Gu, do you think bloggers can successfully elude government censors in repressive nations such as China, Egypt, and Iran? Do you think bloggers in these countries are truly free to express themselves, or are they hemmed in by fear and self-censorship? Defend your answer with quotes from the viewpoints.

2. Jonathan Mirsky argues that Western technology companies are helping China censor its citizens by selling them the technology to block Web sites and filter searches. Clyde Wayne Crews Jr. and Peter Suderman counter that Western tech companies are merely providing technology to the Chinese and should not be blamed if the Chinese government uses that technology to censor its citizens. Do you believe Google, Yahoo, and other companies should get out of China until the Chinese government improves its human rights record? Or will their presence improve human rights in the long run? Explain your answer.

Chapter 4

1. After reading the viewpoint by Debra Lau Whelan, do you believe that self-censorship among librarians is a serious problem? Why or why not? Do you believe you have access to the reading materials you want to read? Explain.

2. Have you read any books on the American Library Association's list of challenged books? Do you believe

these books should be removed from the library? Why or why not?

3. After reading the viewpoints by Debra J. Saunders and Daniel Henninger, do you think the U.S. Supreme Court made the right decision in the "Bong Hits 4 Jesus" case? Why or why not? Do you think students deserve the same speech rights as adults? Use references to the viewpoints to support your answers.

4. Based on your reading of the viewpoints by Nat Hentoff and Bill Frist, do you believe the flag desecration amendment should be passed? Would banning flag desecration violate the very freedom the flag represents, or would it enshrine that freedom by protecting its most potent symbol? Explain.

Organizations to Contact

The editors have compiled the following list of organizations concerned with the issues debated in this book. The descriptions are derived from materials provided by the organizations. All have publications or information available for interested readers. The list was compiled on the date of publication of the present volume; the information provided here may change. Be aware that many organizations take several weeks or longer to respond to inquiries, so allow as much time as possible.

American Civil Liberties Union (ACLU)

125 Broad Street, 18th Floor, New York, NY 10004
(212) 549-2500 • fax: (212) 549-2646
e-mail: aclu@aclu.org
Web site: www.aclu.org

The American Civil Liberties Union (ACLU) is a national organization that defends Americans' civil rights as guaranteed in the U.S. Constitution. It advocates for freedom of all forms of speech, including pornography, flag burning, and political protest. The ACLU offers numerous reports, fact sheets, and policy statements on free speech issues on its Web site. Some of these publications include *Reclaiming Our Rights: Declaration of First Amendment Rights and Grievances*, *Free Speech Under Fire*, and *Freedom of Expression*.

American Library Association (ALA)

50 East Huron Street, Chicago, IL 60611
(800) 545-2433 • fax: (312) 440-9374
e-mail: ala@ala.org
Web site: www.ala.org

The American Library Association (ALA) is the primary professional organization for librarians in the United States. Through its Office for Intellectual Freedom (OIF), the ALA supports free access to libraries and library materials. The OIF also monitors and opposes efforts to ban books from libraries. Its publications, which are available on its Web site, include *Intellectual Freedom and Censorship Q & A*, *Library Bill of Rights*, and *Freedom to Read Statement*.

Concerned Women for America (CWA)

1015 Fifteenth Street NW, Suite 1100, Washington, DC   20005
(202) 488-7000 • fax: (202) 488-0806
Web site: www.cwfa.org

Concerned Women for America (CWA) is a public policy women's organization that promotes Christian values. One of its six major areas of focus is opposition to pornography. Its publications include the monthly *Family Voice* magazine, which contains articles on Internet pornography and filtering software, including "Filters in Libraries: Protecting Our Kids."

Electronic Frontier Foundation (EFF)

454 Shotwell Street, San Francisco, CA   94110-1914
(415) 436-9333 • fax (415) 436-9993
e-mail: information@eff.org
Web site: www.eff.org

Electronic Frontier Foundation (EFF) is a nonprofit organization that works to protect privacy, freedom of speech, and other rights in the digital world. Fighting censorship on the Internet is one of its core missions. Its publications, which are available on its Web site, include *Legal Guide for Bloggers* and white papers such as "Avoiding Gripes About Your Gripe (or Parody) Site," and "Noncommercial Email Lists: Collateral Damage in the Fight Against Spam."

Fairness & Accuracy in Reporting (FAIR)

112 West Twenty-seventh Street, New York, NY   10001
(212) 633-6700 • fax: (212) 727-7668
e-mail: fair@fair.org
Web site: www.fair.org

Fairness & Accuracy in Reporting (FAIR) is a nonprofit media watchdog organization that monitors the press and points out what it claims are biases, inaccuracies, and cases of censorship. FAIR is a politically progressive organization that opposes large media conglomerates and advocates independent public broadcasting. It publishes the magazine *Extra!* which contains articles and commentaries on censorship, including "From Self-Censorship to Official Censorship: Ban on Images of Wounded GIs Raises No Media Objections," "When the White House Says Hush: Treating the 'State Secrets Privilege' as Classified Information," and "Network News Blackout on Pentagon Pundits."

Family Research Council (FRC)

801 G Street NW, Washington, DC   20001
(202) 393-2100 • fax: (202) 393-2134
Web site: www.frc.org

The Family Research Council (FRC) is a nonprofit organization that promotes public policies that are based on Christian values and that endorse traditional families. It believes that pornography harms women, children, and families and seeks to strengthen current obscenity laws. FRC publishes books, policy papers, fact sheets, and other materials, including the brochures *Internet Guide for Parents* and *Dealing with Pornography: A Practical Guide for Protecting Your Family and Your Community* and the book *Protecting Your Child in an X-Rated World: What You Need to Know to Make a Difference.*

Federal Communications Commission (FCC)

445 Twelfth Street SW, Washington, DC   20554
(888) 225-5322 • fax: (866) 418-0232
e-mail: fccinfo@fcc.gov
Web site: www.fcc.gov

The Federal Communications Commission (FCC) is a government agency responsible for regulating telecommunications. Among its other duties, it enforces federal laws related to broadcast indecency. The FCC publishes reports, updates, and reviews on its Web site, including the fact sheets "Obscene, Indecent, and Profane Broadcasts" and "Children's Internet Protection Act."

Foundation for Individual Rights in Education (FIRE)

601 Walnut Street, Suite 510, Philadelphia, PA 19106
(215) 717-3473 • fax: (215) 717-3440
e-mail: fire@thefire.org
Web site: www.thefire.org

The Foundation for Individual Rights in Education (FIRE) was founded in 1999 to defend the rights of students and professors at American colleges and universities. The group advocates for and provides legal assistance to students and professors who feel that their individual rights, particularly their right to free speech, have been violated. Its publications include *FIRE's Guide to Free Speech on Campus* and the *FIRE Quarterly* newsletter. Its Web site features a searchable database called Spotlight that contains information about speech codes at specific colleges and universities.

Free Expression Policy Project (FEPP)

170 West Seventy-sixth Street, Suite 301, New York, NY 10023
(212) 998-6733 • fax: (212) 995-4550
e-mail: margeheins@verizon.net
Web site: www.fepproject.org

The Free Expression Policy Project (FEPP) is a project of the Democracy Program at New York University School of Law's Brennan Center for Justice. FEPP promotes freedom of expression in a "non-absolutist" fashion. It believes that certain forms of speech, such as harassing and threatening speech, are not entitled to First Amendment protection. Its publications include fact sheets, commentaries, and policy reports, which are available on its Web site. Titles include "Fact Sheet on Political Dissent and Censorship," the policy report "Intellectual Property and Free Speech in the Online World," and the commentary "Free Speech in the Age of Obama: Proposals for Year 1." Marjorie Heins is the founder and director of the Free Expression Policy Project.

Free Speech Coalition (FSC)

PO Box 10480, Canoga Park, CA   91309
(818) 348-9373 • fax: (818) 886-5914
Web site: www.freespeechcoalition.com

The Free Speech Coalition (FSC) is a trade association that represents members of the adult entertainment industry. It seeks to protect the industry from attempts to censor pornography. Its publications include the journal *Free Speaker* and various reports and industry press releases.

Freedom Forum

1101 Wilson Boulevard, Arlington, VA   22209
(703) 528-0800 • fax: (703) 284-3770
e-mail: news@freedomforum.org
Web site: www.freedomforum.org

The Freedom Forum was founded in 1991 to defend a free press and free speech. It operates the Newseum (a museum of news and the news media) and the First Amendment Center, which works to educate the public about free speech and other First Amendment issues. Its publications include an annual "State of the First Amendment" survey. The First Amendment Center maintains a First Amendment Library on its Web site, which serves as a clearinghouse for judicial, legislative, and other materials on First Amendment freedoms.

International Freedom of Expression eXchange(IFEX)

IFEX Clearing House
c/o Canadian Journalists for Free Expression (CJFE)
555 Richmond Street West, Suite 1101, PO Box 407
Toronto, ON   M5V 3B1
   Canada
(416) 515-9622 • fax: (416) 515-7879

e-mail: ifex@ifex.org
Website: www.ifex.org

International Freedom of Expression eXchange (IFEX) is a group of more than eighty organizations operating in over fifty countries to promote and protect the free flow of information and freedom of expression. Its work is coordinated by the Toronto-based Clearing House. Through the Action Alert Network, organizations report abuses of free expression to the Clearing House, which distributes the information throughout the world. Publications include the weekly newsletter *Communiqué*, which reports on free expression triumphs and violations, and the twice-weekly *IFEX Digest*, a compilation of news items related to free expression.

Morality in Media, Inc. (MIM)
475 Riverside Drive, Suite 239, New York, NY   10115
(212) 870-3222 • fax: (212) 870-2765
e-mail: mim@moralityinmedia.org
Web site: www.moralityinmedia.org

Morality in Media, Inc. (MIM) is a national interfaith organization that fights obscenity and indecency in the media. It works to educate the public on obscenity issues and maintains the National Obscenity Law Center, a clearinghouse of legal materials on obscenity law. Its publications include the reports *Social Costs of Pornography* and *Pornography's Effects on Adults and Children* and the quarterly *Morality in Media Newsletter*.

National Coalition Against Censorship (NCAC)
275 Seventh Avenue, Suite 1504, New York, NY   10001
(212) 807-6222 • fax: (212) 807-6245
e-mail: ncac@ncac.org
Web site: www.ncac.org

The National Coalition Against Censorship (NCAC) is an alliance of more than fifty national organizations dedicated to protecting access to information and freedom of expression. It provides resources and support to individuals and organizations responding to incidents of censorship; educates and empowers the public to fight censorship; provides documents and reports on current censorship issues; expands public awareness of the prevalence of censorship and suppression of information; and works to influence judicial opinions about free expression and access to information. The NCAC Web site provides access to press releases, legal briefs, and congressional testimony on censorship issues. Its publications include the quarterly *NCAC Censorship News*, the booklet *Public Education, Democracy, Free Speech: The Ideas That Define and Unite Us*, and the book *Censoring Culture: Contemporary Threats to Free Expression*.

National Coalition for the Protection of Children & Families

800 Compton Road, Suite 9224, Cincinnati, OH   45231
(513) 521-6227 • fax: (513) 521-6337
e-mail: ncpcf@nationalcoalition.org
Web site: www.nationalcoalition.org

The National Coalition for the Protection of Children & Families is a Christian organization that encourages traditional sexual ethics and fights pornography. It encourages strong regulation of adult bookstores and the use of Internet filters in public libraries. Its publications include the monthly newsletter *Action*, the resource package *Library Protection Plan*, and the booklet *Pornography: The Deconstruction of Human Society*.

People for the American Way (PFAW)

2000 M Street NW, Suite 400, Washington, DC   20036
(202) 467-4999 • fax: (202) 293-2672
Web site: www.pfaw.org

People for the American Way (PFAW) is a nonprofit organization that promotes citizen participation in democracy and works to safeguard the principles of the U.S. Constitution, including the right to free speech. It publishes a variety of fact sheets, articles, and position statements on its Web site, including the articles "Schools and Censorship" and "Back to School with the Religious Right."

Reporters Without Borders (RWB)

1500 K Street NW, Suite 600, Washington, DC   20005
(202) 256-5613
e-mail: clc@rsf.org
Web site: www.rsf.org

Reporters Without Borders (RWB) is an international organization that advocates press freedom worldwide. It defends imprisoned and tortured journalists; fights against censorship and laws that undermine press freedom; gives financial aid to journalists, media outlets in difficulty, and families of imprisoned journalists; and works to improve the safety of journalists, especially those reporting in war zones. The organization's Web site offers press releases and reports and maintains a daily list of journalists killed or imprisoned around the world. Each year, it publishes "The Worldwide Press Freedom Index," which ranks the nations of the world on the basis of freedom of the press.

Rutherford Institute

PO Box 7482, Charlottesville, VA   22906-7482
(434) 978-3888 • fax: (434) 978-1789
email: staff@rutherford.org
Web site: www.rutherford.org

The Rutherford Institute is a conservative organization that was founded to defend First Amendment rights, including the right to freedom of speech and freedom of religion. The institute provides free legal aid to people who believe that their rights to these freedoms have been violated. The Rutherford Institute's publications, which are available on its Web site, include the commentaries "Edging Near to Dictatorship?" and "Flag Amendment Violates Free Speech" and the white paper "Through the Looking Glass: What Are Young People Learning from Unconstitutional Religious Censorship?"

Bibliography of Books

Harold Abelson, Ken Ledeen, and Harry Lewis — *Blown to Bits: Your Life, Liberty, and Happiness After the Digital Explosion.* Upper Saddle River, NJ: Addison-Wesley, 2008.

M. Shahid Alam — *Challenging the New Orientalism: Dissenting Essays on the "War Against Islam."* North Haledon, NJ: Islamic Publications International, 2006.

Bettina Aptheker — *Intimate Politics: How I Grew Up Red, Fought for Free Speech, and Became a Feminist Rebel.* Emeryville, CA: Seal Press, 2006.

Robert Atkins and Svetlana Mintcheva, eds. — *Censoring Culture: Contemporary Threats to Free Expression.* New York: New Press, 2006.

Fernando Báez — *A Universal History of the Destruction of Books: From Ancient Sumer to Modern Iraq.* New York: Atlas, 2008.

David Dadge, ed. — *Silenced: International Journalists Expose Media Censorship.* Amherst, NY: Prometheus, 2005.

David Dadge — *The War in Iraq and Why the Media Failed Us.* Westport, CT: Praeger, 2006.

Alan M. Dershowitz — *Finding Jefferson: A Lost Letter, a Remarkable Discovery, and the First Amendment in an Age of Terrorism.* Hoboken, NJ: John Wiley & Sons, 2008.

Thomas Patrick Doherty	*Hollywood's Censor: Joseph I. Breen & the Production Code Administration.* New York: Columbia University Press, 2007.
Donald Alexander Downs	*Restoring Free Speech and Liberty on Campus.* New York: Cambridge University Press, 2005.
Garrett Epps, ed.	*The First Amendment, Freedom of the Press: Its Constitutional History and the Contemporary Debate.* Amherst, NY: Prometheus, 2008.
Christopher M. Finan	*From the Palmer Raids to the Patriot Act: A History of the Fight for Free Speech in America.* Boston, MA: Beacon, 2007.
Ernest Freeberg	*Democracy's Prisoner: Eugene V. Debs, the Great War, and the Right to Dissent.* Cambridge, MA: Harvard University Press, 2008.
James LaRue	*The New Inquisition: Understanding and Managing Intellectual Freedom Challenges.* Westport, CT: Libraries Unlimited, 2007.
Robert A. Levy and William H. Mellor	*The Dirty Dozen: How Twelve Supreme Court Cases Radically Expanded Government and Eroded Freedom.* New York: Sentinel, 2008.
Andrew P. Napolitano	*A Nation of Sheep.* Nashville, TN: Thomas Nelson, 2007.
Sara Paretsky	*Writing in an Age of Silence.* London: Verso, 2007.

John Durham Peters — *Courting the Abyss: Free Speech and the Liberal Tradition*. Chicago: University of Chicago Press, 2005.

Lucien X. Polastron — *Books on Fire: The Destruction of Libraries Throughout History*. Trans. Jon E. Graham. Rochester, VT: Inner Traditions, 2007.

Richard A. Posner — *Not a Suicide Pact: The Constitution in a Time of National Emergency*. New York: Oxford University Press, 2006.

Toni Samek — *Librarianship and Human Rights: A Twenty-First Century Guide*. Oxford, UK: Chandos, 2007.

Geoffrey R. Stone — *Perilous Times: Free Speech in Wartime from the Sedition Act of 1798 to the War on Terrorism*. New York: W.W. Norton, 2004.

David Wallis, ed. — *Killed Cartoons: Casualties from the War on Free Expression*. New York: W.W. Norton, 2007.

Rick Wartzman — *Obscene in the Extreme: The Burning and Banning of John Steinbeck's The Grapes of Wrath*. New York: PublicAffairs, 2008.

Shirley A. Wiegand and Wayne A. Wiegand — *Books on Trial: Red Scare in the Heartland*. Norman, OK: University of Oklahoma Press, 2007.

John Ziegler   *The Death of Free Speech: How Our*
                      Broken National Dialogue Has Killed
                      the Truth and Divided America.
                      Nashville, TN: Cumberland House,
                      2005.

PROPERTY OF
HIGH POINT PUBLIC LIBRARY
HIGH POINT, N. C. 27261

Index

A

Abbas, Wael, 103–104
ABC News, 30
Abortion in art, 40, 42
Abu Ghraib prison scandal, 15, 16
ACLU (American Civil Liberties Union), 14, 15, 16
Across the River and into the Trees (Hemingway), 152
Afghanistan conflict
  abuses, coverage, 14, 34
  journalism dangers, 95
  surveillance stories withheld, 37
Age verification, Internet, 66–67
Air America, 177, 179
Al-Farhan, Fouad, 107
al-Qaeda, 30–31
al-Zahar, Mahmoud, 23
Alito, Samuel, 163
Alternative views, net neutrality debate, 85
Amendment process, 168, 173–174, 175
American Civil Liberties Union (ACLU), 14, 15, 16
American flag. *See* Flag desecration amendment proposal
American Library Association (ALA)
  commentary, book banning, 144
  most-challenged book list, 147, 154–155
An American Tragedy (Dreiser), 152

And Tango Makes Three (Parnell and Richardson), 149
Anti-American sentiment, 15–16
Anti-flag desecration amendment. *See* Flag desecration amendment proposal
Anti-*Hazelwood* laws, 140–141
Anti-Islamic views
  perceived in art, 47
  press should not self-censor, 54–59
  press should self-censor, 49–53
Anti-terrorism efforts
  censorship needed to protect, 21, 23–24, 26–27, 29–31
  censorship not needed, 32, 33–38
  domestic surveillance programs, 27–28
Antiwar films, 22
Artists' rights, 79
Arts
  should be censored, 39–43
  should not be censored, 44–48, 56
  theatre censorship examples, 45

B

Backlin, Jim, 85
Balzac, Honoré de, 153
Bandwith, 75–76, 90
Banned books. *See* Book banning
Baquet, Dean, 32–38
Barber, Nigel, 153

Behzti (play), 47, 48

Berg, Nicholas, 16

Bethel School District v. Fraser (1986), 163

Bill of Rights, 168

Billboard Music Awards, 19

Birmingham Repertory Theatre, 47, 48

Black, Hugo, 34

Blankley, Tony, 21–31

Blanshard, Paul, 152

Blocking, Internet content
China, 102, 113, 114–121, 125, 129, 134, 135
repressive governments, general, 96, 97, 98–99
See also Internet; Internet filtering mechanisms

Blogs and blogging
censorship evasion, 106–112, 122, 123–126
freedom-granting, 124
international censorship, 99, 101–102, 103, 118, 119–120, 124–125, 134
regulations, 99, 125, 126
self-censorship, 118, 119, 120, 122, 126–127

Blume, Judy, 145–146

Bond, Edward, 45

Bono, 19

Book banning
historical, U.S., 152–154
is declining in the U.S., 150–155
is happening in the U.S., 142–149

Book burning, 151, 154

Book reading habits, 155

Booth, Coe, 147–148

Boston, Rob, 150–155

Bottlenecks, Internet, 114–115

Box Out (Coy), 148

Boy Meets Boy (Levithan), 149

Boy Toy (Lyga), 143–144

Boycotts, 51

Brannen, Sarah S., 149

Breyer, Stephen, 165–166

Broadband services, 75–76, 77–78, 89, 90, 91
See also Internet service providers

Burger, Warren, 182

Bush, George W.
anti-flag desecration amendment, 168
media criticisms, 29, 31, 34
non-transparency policy, 15
terrorist surveillance programs, 27–28

Businesses
American, abetting Chinese Internet censorship, 128–132
American, promotion of Chinese Internet freedom, 133–136
China, censorship workarounds, 116–117

Byrd, Robert, 169

C

Cakes and Ale (Maugham), 152

Canada, 52

Cannery Row (Steinbeck), 152

Carter, Jimmy, 26

The Catcher in the Rye (Salinger), 154–155

Catholic Church, 152–154

Center for American Progress, 176, 180–186

Center for Safe and Responsible Internet Use, 69

Central Intelligence Agency programs, press coverage, 30, 37

Cerf, Vint, 91

Chacha and Jingjing, 101–102

Chamberlain, Lord, 45

Cher, 19

Child Online Protection Act (COPA) (1998), 62–63, 65–67

Children
    dangers, net neutrality, 74–78
    protections, Internet filters, 63, 64–67, 68–73
    protections, Internet regulations, 62–63, 65–67, 69–72
    television, protection from inappropriate content, 19

Children's Internet Protection Act (CIPA) (2000), 63, 69–71

Children's/young adult literature censorship, 142, 143–149, 151, 154

China
    American technologies abetting Internet censorship, 128–132
    American technologies promoting Internet freedom, 125, 133–136
    cultural insularity, 114, 118–119, 120–121, 131
    flag desecration laws, 171
    Internet censorship can be circumvented, 122–127, 134–135
    Internet censorship described, 96, 97, 98, 99, 100–102, 104, 124–125, 134
    Internet censorship is effective, 113–121
    "mental firewall," 118

Choke points, Internet, 114–115

Christian Coalition of America, 75, 77

Cisco Systems, and Chinese Internet censorship, 130, 133

Citadel Broadcasting Corp., 181

Civil liberties infringement, wartime, 23–25, 27–28

Civil War, 25

Climate change debate, 91–92

Commercial radio, 81, 184–185
    See also Talk radio

Commercial Web sites, regulation, 66–67

Communications Decency Act (CDA) (1996), 62, 65

Community standards, language, 19

Comstock, Anthony, 152

Conason, Joe, 24

Conda, Cesar, 74–78

Congress
    flag protection amendment, con- stance, 167–171
    flag protection amendment, pro- stance, 172–175
    Internet regulation to protect children, 62–63, 65–67, 69–72, 74–78
    net neutrality, con- stances, 75, 76–78, 88–92
    net neutrality, pro- stance, 79–87

Conservatives
    criticisms of net neutrality, 75, 77–78, 88–92
    support of net neutrality, 85

talk radio programs and Fairness Doctrine, 176, 177, 178–179, 180, 181, 182, 183, 184
See also Fundamentalist religious groups
Constitutional amendments, anti-flag desecration. *See* Flag desecration amendment proposal
Constitutional history, 168–169, 174
Consumer boycotts, 51
Cooke, Dominic, 44–48
Coy, John, 148
Crews, Clyde Wayne, Jr., 133–136
Critique of Pure Reason (Kant), 153
Cuba, 171

D

Danish political cartoons controversy, 2005-2006, 49–53, 54–59
Data mining, 104–105
Data packet monitoring, 100, 114–115
Dean, Katy, 140
Dean v. Utica Community Schools (2004), 140–141
Declaration of Independence, 57
Deleting Online Predators Act (DOPA) (bill), 63
Department of Defense. *See* U.S. Department of Defense
Des Moines Independent Community School District, Tinker v. (1969). *See Tinker v. Des Moines Independent Community School District* (1969)
Discipline, schools, 164–166

Dissent
freedoms squelched by Patriot Act, 23–24
World War I policies, 24–25
See also Blogs and blogging
Diverse voices
media consolidation debate, 177–178, 179, 180, 181, 182, 183, 185–186
net neutrality debate, 85
DoD. *See* U.S. Department of Defense
Dodd, Christopher, 28
Domestic surveillance
citizen Internet activity, 96, 97, 98–105, 115, 119–120, 125, 129, 130
National Security Agency wiretapping, 27–28, 37
Patriot Act provisions, 24
Dreiser, Theodore, 152
Drug use and student speech, 156–160, 161–166
Dynamic filtering, Internet, 67, 71, 102

E

e-Keep the Internet Decent and Safe (e-KIDS) Act (bill), 72
E-mail
Internet freedom applications, 109, 117, 118, 135
surveillance, 102, 104
E-Rate program, 69
Early Morning (play), 45
Education, Internet safety, 72–73
Educational materials blocking, 63, 65–66, 69–71, 152
Egypt, Internet censorship, 96, 97, 98, 102, 103–104, 107

Electronic Frontier Foundation (EFF), 62

Electronic surveillance
citizen Internet activity, 96, 97, 98–105, 115, 119–120, 125, 129, 130
domestic wiretapping, 27–28, 37

Ellsworth, Brad, 72

Elmer Gantry (Lewis), 152

Equal time regulations. *See* Fairness Doctrine (FCC)

Evolution, censorship in education, 152

Explicit language
books, 148
television, 19–20

F

Fadlallah, Muhammad Hussein, 23

Fairness Doctrine (FCC)
alternatives to replace, 181–186
criticisms, 176, 177–179
history, 176, 178, 180, 182, 183
misconceptions, 181–182, 183

Fallows, James, 113–121

Farber, David, 90

Fatah, 52

Faulkner, William, 152

Federal Communications Commission (FCC)
Fairness Doctrine, 176, 177–179, 180, 181–186
Internet regulation proposals, 77
live broadcasting regulations, 19–20

Feingold, Russ, 28

Fiction. *See* Book banning; Literature

Films, antiwar, 22

Filtering software, 63
is effective, 64–67
is ineffective, 68–73
See also Internet filtering mechanisms

Finley, Karen, 40

Firewalls. *See* Blocking, Internet content; "Great Firewall of China"

First Amendment rights
broadcasting values, 19–20, 185–186
flag desecration, 167, 168–171, 174
high school journalism, 140–141
Internet content, 62–63, 90, 92
protections exceptions, 139, 174
review of protections, 26
student speech, 139, 156–160, 161–166

FISA court warrants, 27, 34

Flag desecration amendment proposal
does not threaten freedom (pro- stance), 172–175
outcome, 167, 174
threatens freedom (con- stance), 167–171

Flaubert, Gustave, 153, 154

Fleeting expletives, 19–20

Foreign Intelligence Surveillance Act (FISA), 27–28

Fortas, Abraham, 158

Fowler, Geoffrey A., 118

Fox Broadcasting, 19

France, press, 52
Fraser, Bethel School District v. (1986), 163
Frederick, Joseph, 156, 157–160, 162–163
Frederick, Morse v. (2007), 156, 157–160, 161, 162–163
Free artistic expression, 39, 42–43, 46–47
Free market values, 178, 179, 181
Freedom of expression, students, 139, 158
Freedom of Information Act, 14
Freedom of speech
  defined, 57
  does not apply to students, 164
  international values differences, 96
  United States, 139
  See also First Amendment rights; Student speech
Freedom of the press, 34, 49, 52, 55, 95–96
  See also Press
Frist, Bill, 172–175
Fundamentalist religious groups
  art censorship, 44, 47
  book censorship, 151, 152, 155
Future of Music Coalition, 84

G

Gao Yaojie, 123
Gaskill, William, 45
Gay literature, 148–149, 155
Geller, Henry, 185
Germany, press, 52
Gibbon, Edward, 153
Gingrich, Newt, 26

Goldberg, Jonah, 24–25
Golden Globe Awards, 19
Golden Shield Project (China), 114, 115, 119
Google
  Chinese Internet censorship and, 128, 130, 131, 133, 134, 135, 136
  net neutrality opinion, 89–90, 91
  services and applications, 135
"Great Firewall of China," 96, 97, 102, 113, 114–121
  See also China
Gu, April, 122–127

H

Habeas corpus, suspension, 25
Hajdu, David, 154
Hamas, 23, 26
Harassment. *See* Internet harassment; Judicial harassment
Harris, Will, 66
Harry Potter series (Rowling), 151
Hate speech
  freedom of the press vs., 52, 53, 55
  as non-protected speech, 174
Hazelwood School District et al. v. Kuhlmeier et al. (1988), 140–141, 163
Helms, Jesse, 41
Hemingway, Ernest, 152
Henninger, Daniel, 161–166
Hentoff, Nat, 167–171
Hezbollah, 23
High school journalism, 139, 140–141

The Higher Power of Lucky (Patron), 145

The History of the Decline and Fall of the Roman Empire (Gibbon), 153

Hoekstra, Peter, 57

Homosexual literature, 148–149, 155

Hoover, J. Edgar, 22

Household Internet usage
parental guidance, 66, 67, 78
statistics, U.S., 75–76

Hu Jintao, 131

Hugo, Victor, 153

Human Rights Watch, 16

I

i-SAFE, 72

In loco parentis doctrine, 164–165

Incitement, 15, 49

Indecent speech
defined, television, 19
Internet regulation attempts, 62
See also Explicit language

Index Librorum Prohibitorum, 153–154

Intelligence Community Whistleblower Protection Act (1998), 27

Intelligence gathering, 27–29, 30–31

International Society for Technology in Education, 72–73

Internet
al-Qaeda communications systems, 30–31
American usage statistics, 75, 76

censorship, repressive countries, 96, 97–105, 113–121, 124–125

censorship evasion, repressive countries, 106–112, 122–127, 134–135

censorship issues and American technology, 128–132, 133–136

economic development/ benefits, 75, 76, 77, 80, 85, 91, 135–136

music industry and, 79–87

nationalization, 89–92

neutrality laws may cause censorship, 88–92

neutrality laws will endanger families, 74–78

neutrality laws will prevent censorship, 79–87

regulation history, 62–63, 65–67, 69, 70, 72, 76–77

world usage statistics, 107, 110, 134

Internet cafés, 99, 103

Internet commerce, 154

Internet filtering mechanisms, 63
are effective, 64–67
are ineffective, 68–73
net neutrality nullification, 74, 77
state censorship, 98–99, 128–132

Internet Freedom Preservation Act (bill), 76–77

Internet harassment, 63, 68, 72, 102–103

Internet police, 101–102, 125

Internet predators, 68, 70

Internet safety
parents, 66, 67
school environment, 72–73

Internet service providers
    censorship and, 104, 114–115, 118, 119, 120
    net neutrality, con- stance, 74, 77–78, 89, 90
    net neutrality, pro- stance, 79, 86
Investment, Internet technology, 88, 91
Iran
    flag desecration laws, 171
    intelligence activity, 30
    Internet censorship, 96, 98
Iraq, blogging, 108–109, 111–112
Iraq War, 2003-
    abuses, coverage, 14–16, 34
    blogging coverage, 108–109
    media opinions, 25–26
    WMDs issue, 31, 34
Islam. *See* Anti-Islamic views
ISPs. *See* Internet service providers
Israeli-Lebanese conflict, 2006, 109, 111

J

Japanese internment, 25
Jibberwillies at Night (Vail), 146
Jingjing and Chacha, 101–102
Journalists. *See* Press
Joyce, James, 153
Judicial harassment, 96
Juste, Carsten, 51
Jyllands-Posten (Danish newspaper), 49–53, 54–59

K

Kahn, Robert, 90
Kaiser, Robert G., 35
Kant, Immanuel, 153

Keller, Bill, 29, 32–38
Kerpen, Phil, 88–92
Keyword-tracking technologies, 102, 104, 129, 130, 134
Kimball, Roger, 14
King, Peter T., 28–29
Kleinfeld, Andrew, 159
Koh, Terence, 46–47
Koran, 56
Kristof, Nicholas D., 135
Kuhlmeier et al., Hazelwood School District et al. v. (1988), 140–141, 163
Kulash, Damian, 79–87
Kushner, Adam B., 97–105

L

L.A. Times
    CIA program reporting, 30
    editors' opinions on wartime censorship, 32–38
    government surveillance coverage, 33, 35, 37–38
Lady Chatterley's Lover (Lawrence), 153
Lan Chengzhang, 123
Latham, John, 56
Lawrence, D.H., 153
League of United Latin American Citizens (LULAC), 184
Leaks, national security information, 26–27, 28–31, 30
Lebanese-Israeli conflict, 2006, 109, 111
Lee, Euna, 95
Leedom-Ackerman, Joanne, 101
Left-leaning talk radio, 177–178, 179, 180

Legislation. *See* Congress; specific legislation

Les Misérables (Hugo), 153

Lessig, Larry, 91

Levithan, David, 149

Lewis, Sinclair, 152

Libraries

book banning, 142, 143–145, 146–149, 150, 155

Internet filtering, 63, 69, 70, 72

See also Schools and the Internet

Library user records, 24

Licenses, broadcasting, 178, 182, 184–185

Limbaugh, Rush, 179, 181, 183, 184

Lincoln, Abraham, 25

Lindman, Pia, 42

Ling, Laura, 95

Literature

adult, censorship history, 152–155

children's/YA, censorship, 142–149, 151

Live television broadcasting, 19–20

Lloyd, Mark, 180–186

Local media ownership/input, 177, 180, 181, 182, 184, 185–186

Lockwood, Alex, 91–92

LULAC (League of United Latin American Citizens), 184

Lyga, Barry, 143–144

M

MacKinnon, Rebecca, 119, 121, 131–132

Madame Bovary (Flaubert), 153, 154

Mainstream media. *See* Press

Mapplethorpe, Robert, 41, 43

Markey, Edward, 76–77

Marx, Karl, 108

Marzook, Mousa Abu, 23

Maugham, W. Somerset, 152

May, Gary, 169

May, Randolph J., 90

Media ownership and consolidation, 177–178, 180, 181–186

Medical language blockage, Internet, 62, 71, 99

Microsoft

Chinese Internet censorship and, 128, 130, 131, 134, 136

MSN Spaces blog, 125

Middle East

Internet censorship, 102–104

Internet censorship evasion, 106, 107–108, 108–109, 111–112

Internet usage statistics, 107, 110

Mill, John Stuart, 153

Minors. *See* Children

Mirroring, Internet data, 115

Mirsky, Jonathan, 128–132

Morse, Deborah, 156, 157, 159–160, 162

Morse v. Frederick (2007), 156, 157–160, 161, 162–163

MSN Spaces blog, 125

MTV, 81

Muhammad portrayals, *Jyllands-Posten* newspaper, 49–53, 54–59

Music industry and the Internet, 79–87

Music videos, 81, 82–84

N

National Endowment for the Arts (NEA), 41
National secrets. *See* State secrets
National Security Agency (NSA), domestic wiretapping, 27–28, 37
National security issues
  press, voluntary withholding to protect, 33, 35–38
  wartime censorship, con-stance, 32–38
  wartime censorship, pro-stance, 21–31
Nationalization, 89–92
Neutrality, Internet
  laws will endanger families, 74–78
  laws will may cause censor-ship, 88–92
  laws will prevent censorship, 79–87
New York Society for the Suppres-sion of Vice, 152
New York Times
  editors' opinions on wartime censorship, 29, 32–38
  government surveillance cov-erage, 27, 28–29, 33, 35, 37–38
  Patriot Act criticisms, 24
North Korea, 95
Norway, 51, 52
Now or Later (play), 48

O

Obama, Barack
  FISA reform vote, 27–28
  net neutrality, 89–90
  war abuses photos, blockage, 14, 15, 16

Obelisk program, 30–31
Obscene content
  art, 39, 40, 41, 42
  Internet, regulation and defin-ing, 62–63
  literature, changing views, 153
Obscene language. *See* Explicit language
Of Mice and Men (Steinbeck), 154–155
Office of Censorship, 22
OK Go, 79, 80, 82–83
Online predators. *See* Internet predators
Online videos, 82–84, 103–104
Op-ed articles, 23
OpenNet Initiative, 102
The Open Society and Its Enemies (Popper), 59
Ownership, stations and licenses, 177–178, 180, 181–186

P

Packet routing, 100, 114–115
Palfrey, John, 129, 131
Panopticon effect, 100–102
Parental involvement
  book disapproval and ban-ning, 142, 145
  Internet use, 66, 67, 78
  schools' parenting role, 164–165
Parnell, Peter, 149
Patriot Act (2001), 24
Patron, Susan, 144–145
Pax, Salam, 111–112
Payola, 81, 84
Pearl, Daniel, 34
Pelley, William Dudley, 23

Pelosi, Nancy, 176, 184

Pentagon Papers, 34

Performance art, 40, 42, 43

Petrocelli, Joseph, 174

Pew Internet & American Life Project, 75, 76

Piracy, 85, 90, 185

Piss Christ (Serrano), 40, 41

Police, Internet, 101–102, 125

Political blogging
Chinese censorship, 118, 123–127
Middle Eastern censorship, 103–104, 106, 107, 108–109, 111–112

Political cartoon portrayals of Muhammad, 2005, 49–53, 54–59

Political speech, flag desecration debate, 167, 172, 174–175

Political talk radio, 176–179, 180–186

Popper, Karl, 59

Pornography
age verification issues, 66–67
Internet, and children, 62
Internet censoring, 98–99, 103
Internet filtering, 64, 65, 70
literature, changing definitions, 153
pay sites, 66

Power aspect of censorship, 16, 24, 34, 45

Pravda (newspaper), 108

Press
blogs as journalism, 106, 108–109, 111, 123, 124, 126
dangers to reporters, 33–34, 123
international freedom/challenges, 95–96, 106

should be censored during wartime, 21–31
should not be censored during wartime, 32–38
should not self-censor anti-Islamic views, 54–59
should self-censor anti-Islamic views, 49–53
withholding stories, national security reasons, 33, 35–38
See also High school journalism

Prisoner abuse, documentation, 15, 16

Promotion, music, 80–85

Protests
Danish political cartoons controversy, 51
flag desecration used, 168, 169–170, 174

Proxy servers, 71, 100, 116, 117, 118

Public broadcasting, 178, 182, 184–185
See also Talk radio

Public forums, 140

Public schools, historic responsibilities, 164–165
See also School book banning; Student speech

Pyne, Joe, 184

Q

Qaeda, al-, 30–31

Quiñones, John, 184

R

Racism and book banning, 148

Radio
commercial, promotions, 81

ownership and consolidation, 177–178, 180, 181–186

regulation of talk radio protects free speech, 180–186

regulation of talk radio threatens free speech, 176–179

Rasmussen, Anders Fogh, 50, 51, 56

Rather, Dan, 36

Reading habits, 155

Reed, Lowell, Jr., 65, 67

Regulation. *See* Congress; Talk radio; specific legislation

Rehnquist, William, 69

Religions, treatment differences, 53, 56, 57–58

Religious groups

art censorship, 44, 47

book censorship, 151, 152–154, 155

free speech protection of students, 157–158

Religiously-based book banning, 148, 150, 151–154, 155

Remote servers, 71, 100, 116, 117, 118

Rendall, Steve, 183

Reporters. *See* Press

Reporters Without Borders, 95–96, 104, 120, 130

Richardson, Justin, 149

Richie, Nicole, 19

The Right to Read: The Battle Against Censorship (Blanshard), 152

"Riverbend," 111

Roberts, John, 163

Rock the Net, 84

The Romans in Britain (play), 40

Roosevelt, Franklin Delano, 22–23, 24, 25

Rose, Flemming, 51, 54–59

Rowling, J.K., 151

Royal Court Theatre, 44, 45, 48

The Royal Smut-Hound (Tynan), 45

Rushdie, Salman, 47

S

Safi, Louay M., 52

Salinger, J.D., 154–155

Sartre, Jean-Paul, 153

Satire, 57–58

Saudi Arabia, Internet censorship, 96, 97, 98–99, 102, 107

Saunders, Debra J., 156–160

Scales, Pat, 144, 146–147

School book banning, 142, 144–145, 146–147, 148, 150, 152, 154–155

School journalism, 139, 140–141

School speech. *See* Student speech

Schools and the Internet, 63, 69–73

Schultz, Ed, 181

Searches, banned terms, 102, 104, 129, 130, 134

Sears, Alan, 176–179

Sedition, 22–23, 24–25

Self-censorship, 148

art world, 42, 44, 47–48

book banning, 144–145, 146, 148, 149

Internet/blogging, 118, 119, 120, 122, 126–127

press should not self-censor anti-Islamic views, 54–59

press should self-censor anti-Islamic views, 49–53

Self-producing, promoting, and publishing, music, 81–82, 82–85

Senate Joint Resolution 12. *See* Flag desecration amendment proposal

Serrano, Andres, 40, 41, 43

Sex education content, 65–66

Sexual content in literature, 143–144, 148, 149, 152, 153

Seymour, Richard, 106–112

Shapiro, Ben, 39–43

Shi Tao, 130

Shinn, Christopher, 48

Shvarts, Aliza, 40, 42, 43

Siddiqui, Haroon, 49–53

Snow, John, 35

Snow, Tony, 29–30

Social networking sites
blocking, censorship challenges, 99–100
blocking, vs. educational use, 63, 69, 70, 73
music promotion, 84

"Soft" censorship, 144

Soliman, Abdel Kareem Nabil, 107

Sonnenblick, Jordan, 148

Starr, Ken, 158–159

State censorship. *See* China; Middle East

State secrets
Chinese Internet censorship charges, 129, 130
wartime and press, 26, 29, 30, 34, 35

Steinbeck, John, 152, 154–155

Sterling, Eric, 158, 159

Stewart, Potter, 14

Streaming content
bandwidth requirements, 75–76, 90
educational, 76
journalistic, 103–104, 109
music, 80, 82–83

"Street lit," 147–148

Student speech
should be censored, 161–166
should not be censored, 139, 156–160
See also High school journalism

Students for Sensible Drug Policy, 158

Subversive literature, 108, 117, 120, 129

Suderman, Peter, 133–136

Sullum, Jacob, 64–67

Sumner, John, 152

Supreme Court, U.S.
FCC regulation cases, 19
flag desecration cases, 173
high school journalism cases, 139, 140, 141
Internet regulation rulings, 62–63, 65, 69
obscenity guidelines, 41
school speech cases, 139, 156–160, 161–166

Surveillance. *See* Domestic surveillance; Intelligence gathering

Swear words. *See* Explicit language

T

Tales of a Fourth Grade Nothing (Blume), 146

Talk radio
regulation will protect free speech, 180–186

regulation will threaten free speech, 176–179

Tao, Mr., 120

Tarnow, Arthur J., 140

Tate Gallery, 56

Taylor, Doug, 151

The Ten-Cent Plague (Hajdu), 154

Terrorists
cartoon portrayals of Muhammad as, 50, 58
Internet use, 30–31
op-eds, American newspapers, 23, 26
surveillance programs, 24, 27–28, 37
See also War on Terror

Theatre, 40, 43, 44, 45–48

Thomas, Clarence, 164–165

Tibet, 98, 99, 100

Tinker v. Des Moines Independent Community School District (1969)
criticisms, 163, 165, 166
Fortas opinion, 158
as precedent case, 139–140, 159

Total Information Awareness project, 104–105

Tynan, Kenneth, 45

Tyrell (Booth), 147–148

U

Ulysses (Joyce), 153

Uncle Bobby's Wedding (Brannen), 149

Underground communication. *See* Blogs and blogging

United States
book banning activity, 142–149
book banning decline, 150–155
book reading habits, 155
companies abetting Chinese Internet censorship, 128–132
companies fighting Chinese Internet censorship, 125
companies promoting Chinese Internet freedom, 133–136
concerns, Chinese Internet censorship, 127

U.S. Department of Defense
Total Information Awareness Project, 104–105
war abuses photos case, 14

Utica Community Schools, Dean v. (2004), 140–141

V

Vail, Rachel, 146

van Gogh, Theo, 51

Vandalism, 172, 174–175

Veterans, flag-burning amendment opinions, 167, 169–170, 170–171

Videos. *See* Web videos

Vietnam, Internet censorship, 97, 99, 100

Vietnam War
press coverage, 34
veterans, 169–170, 170–171

Villano, Matt, 68–73

Virtual Private Networks (VPNs), 116–117, 118

W

War on Terror
censorship needed, 21, 23–24, 26–27, 29–30, 29–31
censorship not needed, 32, 33–38

PROPERTY OF
HIGH POINT PUBLIC LIBRARY
HIGH POINT, N. C. 27261

domestic surveillance programs, 27–28
Warner, James, 169–170
Warrantless wiretaps, 27, 34
Wartime
   press should be censored, 21–31
   press should not be censored, 32–38
Washington Post, 23, 35, 37
Web searching. *See* Searches, banned terms
Web sites. *See* Internet
Web videos
   blogs/journalism, 103–104, 109
   music, 82–84
The West's Last Chance (Blankley), 22
Whelan, Deborah Lau, 142–149
Whistleblowing protocol, 27
Whitehead, John W., 15–16
The Wild Palms (Faulkner), 152
Willard, Nancy, 69–70, 71

Wilson, Woodrow, 24
Women and blogging, 111
World War I, 24–25
World War II, 22, 23, 24, 25
Worldwide Press Freedom Index, 95–96

X

Xia, Bill, 125

Y

Yahoo, and Chinese Internet censorship, 128, 130, 131, 133, 134
Young adult/children's literature censorship, 142, 143–149, 151, 154
YouTube, 83, 103–104

Z

Zahar, Mahmoud al-, 23
Zola, Émile, 153

363.31 Censorsh
Barbour, Scott,
Censorship /2010

PROPERTY OF
HIGH POINT PUBLIC LIBRARY
HIGH POINT, N. C. 27261